Eyewitness to history

"It was terrible. I'm talking about bodies that were piled up and prisoners that looked like skeletons," he said and paused, overcome by the memories 72 years later. "I hate what the enemy did. I couldn't believe man could be so inhumane to other humans."

—Charles J. Palmeri, commenting about what he witnessed at the Dachau concentration camp, as interviewed by Lou Michel, "WWII vet earned Silver Star, but witnessing concentration camp horrors angered him," *The Buffalo News*, July 17, 2017.

What people are saying about *Boy Solider*

Thank you for your service to our country and for your continued commitment to telling the story of World War II. While I was edified by your interview from the May 2020 issue of Columbia, *I greatly appreciate this opportunity to learn more about your life—particularly your experiences during the liberation of Dachau. Please know that I count* Boy Soldier *as an important addition to my library.*

Patrick E. Kelly, Supreme Knight, Knights of Columbus

"...enlightening and moving."
—The Academy at Glengary

"I truly enjoyed reading your book and will cherish it. I was in Vietnam."
—James. J. Schonefeld, Command Sergeant Major (U.S. Army, Retired)

"Thank you for your service and bravery, and for documenting your experiences during such an important time in history."
—Amy Olszewski

"What a wonderful and interesting book!"
—Cella Gutierrez

"Thank you for taking the time to pass this story on to us."
—Sue Ellis

"...thank you for your great service to our nation, which you served so valiantly and with the greatest love for your country, your family, and your faith. God bless you always."
—Doug Mashburn

"Thank you, Chuck, for your service during the war. People like you made it possible for me to grow up in a free America."
—Sue Reiss

"We were very touched by your story and grateful for the sacrifices you made."
—Pat and Shelby Black

"Your willingness to share with all of us was especially great—and gut-wrenching!"
—Beckie Miller

Boy Soldier

Recollections of World War II

Boy Soldier

Recollections of World War II

Charles J. Palmeri

Dedication

Dedicated to the memory of the 42nd Division soldiers who were casualties of over 100 days of fighting in France and Germany during 1944-1945, particularly, Lt. Antonio J. Manniello and Pfc. Clarence E. Fuqua. Both men are buried in France: Lt. Manniello in Épinal, and Pfc. Fuqua in Lorraine Saint-Avold.

Also to Bishop Pius Benincasa, who, as a United States Army Chaplain, landed on Omaha Beach on D-Day.

Acknowledgments

Writing these memoirs of World War II 70 years later would not have been possible without the efforts of family and friends who encouraged me to put the pen to paper.

My thanks to...my daughter, Karin Best, for helping me get my basic notes organized in the initial stages of recall; my niece, Jordan Cosentino, who created the first pages of my book from my many handwritten notes that were written on scraps of paper throughout the years; my wife, Carol, who spent hundreds of hours deciphering, correcting, compiling, and typing the many drafts we did. Carol's conversations with Rainbow veterans during our 50th Anniversary Reunion in Germany, France, and Austria in 1995, seeing the museum at Dachau, and visiting Munich, Wurzburg, Salzburg, Mayerhofen and Büchold (after finding it on a map in a book store in Wurzburg), gave her the insight to draw out memories of my experiences;

the encouragement from my sister, Mary Holland, to preserve these memories for our family; the critiquing of the almost last draft by Maryann and Joe Lisenby for their military input, and John "Jack" Saunders for his dedication in helping me keep my military thoughts in order and being correct. Special thanks to Randy Homack, my sketch artist, for doing a great job on the book cover, and, to my editor, Liz Coursen, for formatting and finalizing my work, and making this book happen.

I want to thank my friend, Robert "Bob" Thornton, for his inspiration in writing this book. Bob was an 8th Air Force B-17 veteran of 35 missions over Germany and received a citation for kicking a 500-pound bomb, which got stuck in the bomb bay, out of his Flying Fortress. He wrote his book, called *Twenty-Seven-Eighty Blues, A Memoir of World War II,* in 1993. Sadly, Bob passed away in March 2019 at the age of 94, but knowing I was close to finishing my book.

Rainbow Songs

"There's a Rainbow in the Army"
(Original Rainbow Song)

There's a Rainbow in the Army,
Like a Rainbow in the sky
Shining brightly in all the glory
Of a past that will not die;

Let our voices show,
In our hearts we know
That the new Rainbow
Will carry on—HEY!

We're the mighty Forty-Second,
And our fathers fought like men,
In the battle now before us
We will fight like they fought then.

With our chins up high
We will win or die—
For the Rainbow in the Army
For the Rainbow in the sky.

"Mountain Dew Song"
(Semi-Official Song)

Down the road here from me
There's an old hollow tree
Where you lay down a dollar or two,
Then you go round the bend
And you come back again
With that good old Mountain Dew.

Oh, they call it that old Mountain Dew
And the ones that refuse it are few.
I will hush up my mug
If you'll fill up my jug
With that good old Mountain Dew.

Preface

I was born the eldest child of five to Joseph C. Palmeri, an immigrant from Sicily, and his American bride, Giovanna Cavaretta, on April 23, 1926, in Buffalo, New York.

I was educated in Catholic schools and desired to be a Catholic priest. I gave up my seminary preparation for the priesthood to join the United States Army in June 1944, to support the war effort, like so many other young men my age. After basic training at Camp Joseph T. Robinson in Little Rock, Arkansas, I went home for a short visit prior to shipping out to the war in Europe.

This is not strictly a war story, it's my story. It's the two-year experience of a young soldier with a little over three months of combat at near war's end with fierce fighting and a high percentage of young American soldier casualties. And this is the story of thirteen months of Army of Occupation duties: (1) viewing the tragedy of the Dachau concentration camp; (2) after war's end (V-E Day) combat patrol; (3) the control and management of a U.S. Army prison camp for over 8,000 Nazi sympathizers from non-German countries—a situation not publicly reported; (4) and, finally, the enjoyment of living in Austria and meeting warm, friendly, and interesting people—particularly, one beautiful young girl.

Three times I miraculously escaped death. I credit my survival to my faith in God and the many prayers said by members of my family during the time I was in Europe.

Pvt. Charles J. Palmeri, United States Army, 1945

42nd Infantry, Rainbow Division Map; note starting point at Marseille and location of Dachau, to the right.

Composition of the WWII
42nd Infantry Division

Three Infantry Regiments: 222nd, 232nd, 242nd

Each Regiment had three Battalions: 1st, 2nd, and 3rd

Each Battalion had four Rifle Companies: ABCD EFGH IKLM. (There is no "J" and I don't know why.)

Each Company had three Rifle Platoons and one Heavy Weapons, plus Company Headquarters departments that include Mess Sergeant, First Sergeant, Clerks, Cooks, Jeep Drivers.

Each Platoon had a leader who was a 2nd Lieutenant, a Sergeant, an Assistant, plus three squads of 12 men each.

Each squad had a Staff Sergeant and Assistant

Each Infantry Division also had:

Medical Dept.

4 Field Artillery Battalions

Engineer Battalion

Signal Company

Ordinance Company

Quarter Master Company

Military Police Platoon

Headquarter Company

Table of Contents

1. Foxhole

My first day on the front lines: Lichtenberg and Alsace-Lorraine in France

It was pitch dark and very cold. Standing in a foxhole several hundred yards from a stream and a path, way beyond the hillside facing me, were German soldiers—they were not visible because of heavy tree foliage. We had just arrived early on the morning of January 30th, 1945, to replace infantrymen of the 45th Division. They were delighted to turn over to us the rather elaborate foxholes that they had dug into the hillside. My new home here was a dugout that was deep back into the hill with a heavy log covering to protect against anything other than a direct hit by artillery or mortar fire. It was a two-room unit with the rear room for one man to

1

sleep while the other stood guard. Unfortunately, I spent this first night on the front lines alone since my buddy Cannon was picked to go on a night patrol with our platoon leader, Lt. Manniello. Manniello had survived a month of tough fighting to protect the city of Strasbourg in Alsace-Lorraine. The Nazi leadership wanted to recapture the city in a battle called Nordland. After the devastating defeat in the Battle of the Bulge, Hitler withdrew from Bastogne, Belgium, sending tanks and infantry south to take Strasbourg. Hitler failed to accomplish his mission because of the staunch defense by a 42nd Division that was new to combat, the 3rd and the 45th Divisions, and a French Moroccan regiment. Manniello made it out alive from a battle that caused fifty percent of Company L's men to be killed, wounded, or captured in a 23-day, snow-covered battle on the Rhine River.

Sgt. Antonio Manniello received a battlefield commission to 2nd Lieutenant after the defense of Strasbourg. He had proved to be a fearless fighter and an exceptional leader during the December 1944 defeat of the German attempt to regain the city. The good looking, very strong, dark-haired Manniello was respected by the platoon soldiers who survived the bitter cold battle.

Now the new Lt. Manniello came to me to explain why I would have to sit in my foxhole alone through my first night on the front lines. He repeated the advice given to us by the

1. Foxhole

departing 45th Division soldiers, who warned that the German soldiers would crawl up our hillside after dark, and yell for help as a wounded American soldier in an attempt to draw us out from our cover. "Stay in your hole," he advised. "Do not leave cover or call out to the 'wounded' man or even acknowledge his presence." I thanked the lieutenant for his advice.

Through the course of that first night, I heard footsteps in the underbrush, experienced flares that lit up the area like daylight, and heard shooting on the German side of "no man's land." It was very scary. In the morning a messenger from Company L's headquarters came to my foxhole location, and to other foxholes to the left and right of mine, wanting to know of any reports of activity. I reported no activity, but learned from him later that, while on the intelligence patrol, Lt. Manniello had been killed by a landmine—his first night in combat as an officer. During our earlier meeting, Lt. Manniello had given me a small Italian-English dictionary to return to him when he got back from the patrol. I still have the dictionary. This was the first, but not the last, crucial experience of the death of a young fellow soldier. It was a crushing awakening that I was no longer "playing" soldier. I wondered, *Who will be next? What can I do to avoid what seems to be the inevitable?*

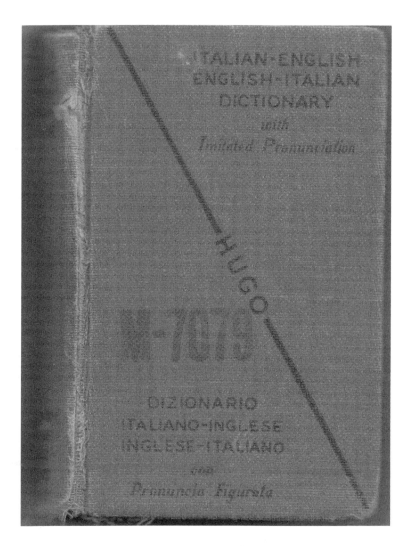

Photos of the cover and interior of Lt. Antonio J. Manniello's Italian-American dictionary

1. Foxhole

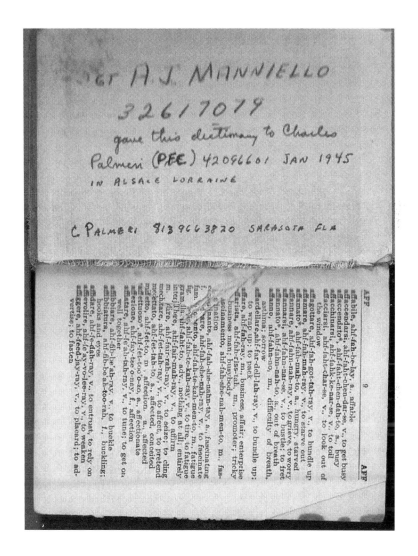

What a terrifying blow. This was my first loss of a comrade in front-line duty. Just hours earlier Lt. Manniello had befriended me, bolstered my morale as a new fearless front-line combatant, and apologized for my having to be alone my first night. Then, in our conversation we had compared his life to mine—both children of Italian American immigrants who worked so hard to raise their boys to be good citizens and now soldiers to fight for America. Lt. Manniello had said to me, "Soon, this will be over and we can return home to college, and then a chance to become a leader in industry or government." But Lt. Antonio Manniello never had a chance. I held his green Italian-American dictionary in my hand and cried—the tears dropping on my platoon leader's little book and thinking his dream of visiting Italy at war's end would never happen. Basic training did not prepare me for this. But looking back to July and Camp Joseph T. Robinson in Little Rock, Arkansas, what did we learn in 17 weeks of basic training to prepare us for a buddy's death?

2. Basic Training: Before Duty

Little Rock, Arkansas, July, 1944

We recruits looked forward to training to become soldiers. While losing personal identity, we learned to obey the commands of superiors, sergeants, and officers. We wore uniforms, shot rifles, and marched to the "hut-hut" of non-commissioned training officers. It took days for many recruits to know their right foot from their left. It was hard work: long hikes, forced marches in 90-degree heat with full packs, crawling through mud and under barbed wire with machine guns firing just inches above our heads, climbing ropes and high walls, throwing live grenades, shooting at moving targets, hand-to-hand and bayonet combat with someone twice your size, putting on a gas mask in a gas-filled room, one hundred pushups and knee bends, sleeping in a pup tent in a rain storm, being awakened at 4:30 a.m. for a V.D. check, then sitting on toilets with ten to twelve other recruits all lined up without any privacy.

We began to feel part of a team of infantry soldiers. We marched with pride on the huge parade ground to the music of an army band, ready to go to war—after we had a short furlough home to show off our new-found military figures in uniform.

But then, on our first pass into Little Rock to see a little civilian life, my buddy, Louis Migliore, from Buffalo, New York, and I wandered the busy main street, then turned onto a side street to avoid heavy traffic. There we met two brightly clad young ladies who asked if we would like to party. I did not want to discourage the girls' patriotic willingness to show support for young soldiers. But Louis, who had worldly experience that was not available to me as a former clergy student, said, "No thanks!" Louis told me, as he pulled me away, that they were hookers. I could not believe my eyes as I looked back at the two girls, smiling at their missed opportunity to ingratiate themselves with two young soldiers. I guess you could call that day part of my training!

2. Basic Training: Before Duty

Charles J. Palmeri at Boot Camp

Louis Migliore at Boot Camp

9

Boy Soldier: Recollections of World War II

3. Furlough and Overseas Trip

I arrive in France.

After 17 weeks of basic training, I returned to Buffalo on December 24th, 1944. I had planned to spend these two weeks of furlough visiting members of our huge Palmeri family and to see two friends, Louise M. and Alice V., who had been keeping my mail calls entertaining, filled with day-to-day Buffalo stories of high school classmates. Sadly, none of these meetings with family and friends took place. Christmas morning, just as mom, dad, and my brother, Vincent, and I returned from church, a phone message from army headquarters ordered me to report to Camp Meade the next day to prepare

11

for immediate shipment to somewhere. The losses in the Battle of the Bulge in Belgium and the defense of Alsace-Lorraine and Strasbourg were so great that replacements were needed to be rushed to the front lines.

We boarded a victory ship, *Mexico Victory*, on New Year's Eve and joined a huge armada of several hundred ships loaded with replacement soldiers, supplies, and armament.

January 1st to January 15th, 1945...14 stormy days at sea. Everyone was seasick. During the day we were allowed on deck for fresh air to alleviate somewhat the *mal de mar*. At night, we had to stay below to avoid the possibility of a soldier lighting a cigarette and giving the German subs a definite target. Often, while trying to destroy enemy subs, the shattering noise and vibration of our Navy depth charges shook our little ship like a toy.

We were fortunate to have as one of our soldiers Hugh Martin, one of the writers of the songs for "Meet Me in St. Louis." Hugh played an upright piano and sang every night, which was a relief from our nightly lockdown. We heard a lot of music and sang songs in the evenings. I vividly remember many songs from this time, including "Praise the Lord and pass the ammunition," "When the caissons go rolling along," and "American Patrol." It was wonderful entertainment from one of our own soldiers.

It was not unusual that a huge wave would hit the ship while I was shaving or washing in

3. Furlough and Overseas Trip

the large latrine area, knocking me down on to the wet tile, causing me to slide to the opposite side of the washroom. Then, when the ship would return on another wave, I would slide back to where I had been, still on hands and knees on the wet tile floor.

After nights of being bounced around by the sea, many sick men refused to eat. However, there were two meals per day. Standing in long lines through areaways filled with a heavy diesel odor just enhanced the dreaded *mal de mar*.

After 15 days of nonstop battle with the sea, I was delighted to see the harbor at Le Havre in France, where long floating docks had been installed out into the harbor to receive us. We carried our duffel bags down the floating docks to set foot on terra firma and into large warehouses. These buildings were called "reppel deppels," slang for "replacement depots." It was there we got medical attention, our new M-1 rifles, and then assignment to an army division. Before moving to our new assignment while in Le Havre, we were served hot meals, saw a movie, and got our first views of the large French city.

Eventually we departed in freight cars called 40+8s (capacity: 40 men or 8 horses). It took two days to reach our destination. The train stopped frequently so we could relieve ourselves, and, at several stations, acquire food. Finally, we transferred to trucks and then to the 42nd Division headquarters, which was on a small French estate in Épinal, a commune in northeastern France. There, we received more warfare training. We fired bazookas, 45-caliber pistols, machine guns and flame throwers, and took long hikes to limber up.

Pvt. Charles J. Palmeri (front), 40+8 Freight Car

4. Company L

On the third day, I was assigned to Company L of the 232nd Regiment in a village named Gramercy. I met the soldiers who had survived the fierce battles defending Strasbourg. There were only 60 battle-weary men to greet us. More than 70 of their buddies had been killed, injured, or captured. Stanley Fusco, Jerry Babich, and other soldiers were there to welcome us to the 3rd Platoon of Company L. They told us stories of their battles at Kilstett and Gamshein. For example, Sgt. Green told us about one battle in December in the Rhine River area where he and a squad were left by his platoon lieutenant at an abandoned "pillbox"—a flat-roofed fortified concrete defense structure used during World Wars I and II as a guard post to defend against

15

powerful artillery, and equipped with holes or slits in the walls from which to fire weapons.

The balance of their platoon continued forward to engage German soldiers trying to cross the Rhine River. The entire forward platoon was wiped out.

The enemy tried to recapture the pillbox without success, but continued to fire at it. Simultaneously, a different Company of the 42nd Division came on the site and began firing at the pillbox, not knowing that the men inside were our soldiers. So, with the enemy attacking from the river's side and Americans firing from the rear, it was so frightening that one young soldier who tried to escape to the rear was shot by the new American force who realized, too late, that the soldier was not German. The American force proceeded to attack the Germans beyond the pillbox, freed up Sgt. Green and his men, and picked up the injured soldier who had tried to escape. There were more stories about battles at the Alsace towns of Gamshein and Kilstett.

We left Gramercy to go to the front line at Lichtenberg. When we were in the truck carrying about 10 of us to the front line area, no one appeared to be overly nervous about heading to the front. There were a few jokes and small talk about pending battle activity until one older man, about 24 years old or so, chastised us for not acknowledging the seriousness of the future danger we faced. I remember he said, "You young guys don't care, but I have a wife and a baby back home. I'm scared I may never see them again." We became quiet and more thoughtful when we saw tears rolling down his cheeks. We departed from the truck, and continued on foot.

On the way we passed a division artillery battalion firing 105 Howitzers into enemy territory. We now knew we were at the war front. To the right of the Lichtenberg castle we followed narrow mountain paths to the foxholes manned by the 45th Division.

Boy Soldier: Recollections of World War II

5. Back in the Foxhole

After the death of Lt. Manniello, we spent another week in our foxholes, with no toilet facilities and only K-rations, which consisted of a 4" x 7" waxed meal box filled with a can of meat, eggs, or cheese; a cracker; a dry coffee mix; and a pack of three cigarettes. We were relieved to return occasionally to Lichtenberg, to sleep in a house, and were treated to real hot food from the regimental kitchen. After a day of rest, our 2nd Platoon's sergeant, Sgt. Beasley, told us we would be going on patrol.

There are two basic kinds of patrol: "intelligence patrol," to determine the location of enemy outposts and headquarters while trying to avoid conflict, and "combat patrol," to engage the enemy to determine his strength and to kill and discourage his soldiers.

We went on two intelligence patrols with Sgt. Beasley. He was fearless leading us into Ruppetsweiler, an almost completely demolished village in no-mans-land, with his Thompson submachine gun slung over his shoulder like he was walking down main street in his home town.

No-mans-land near Ruppetsweiler, France

Neither of these patrols resulted in gunfire, but we learned that the Germans had vacated the area. That was valuable information for the division headquarters planning our advance from defensive line to the offensive, and our march into Germany.

During our second week into defensive positions at Lichtenberg, the 1st Platoon went on a combat patrol into German lines. It met no

5. Back in the Foxhole

opposition until about 3 a.m., when the German rifle fire, from both right and left, cut down several members of our platoon. The platoon sergeant of the 1st Platoon, Sgt. Goldsborough, ordered his men to retreat, but stood his ground, firing his submachine gun to protect the men who were retreating back to our base position. Three men had been killed and several wounded while Sgt. Goldsborough and another soldier, who stayed behind to support him, were captured.

At war's end, in a Munich hospital, members of the 1st Platoon found Sgt. Goldsborough. He had been wounded in the patrol battle along with German soldiers who were also wounded in the same battle. The German soldiers had told our interpreter that they had been very impressed by the bravery of Sgt. Goldsborough in his effort to save his men in retreat.

Several times during those cold nights in our foxholes, German and American flares cast eerie shadows, lighting up the landscape like day. Trees appeared to be enemy soldiers advancing up the hillside from the enemy lines. My first inclination was to shoot at the shadows, but as the flare light began to fade, I realized the shadows were only an illusion. I did not fire.

While on the front lines in Alsace-Lorraine waiting for the push off over the Rhine, we lived in our foxholes. Patrols, brief skirmishes, and artillery and mortar attacks were frequent, so we were surprised and dismayed when our 1st

Sergeant told us to "police-up" the area because an inspector general was coming down from Company Headquarters to check on sanitation and conditions on our front line. We thought that to be unbelievable and ridiculous.

The inspecting officer was with us near our foxholes for only a few minutes when we heard the *shush* of incoming mortar rounds striking a few hundred yards or so between us and the German lines, so we all hit the ground. When a second round hit somewhat closer, the inspector high-tailed it back up the hill and went away. "Inspection time over," I heard our radio operator call back to our weapons platoon. "Last round routed the enemy. It was a little close—over and out."

To relieve the tension of living in a foxhole, the anticipation of enemy activity, and inclement weather, the Division promoted a program of required relaxation for front-line infantrymen. So, in the middle of February, I was granted a two-day rest period at a Division camp: a hot shower, hot meals, I saw a movie, and had a mattress and pillow for a good night's sleep.

We returned by truck to our battalion headquarters to wait for a Jeep ride back to Lichtenberg and the reality of foxhole living.

While waiting for the Jeep, I needed to visit a latrine. There was a house and an outbuilding. I was directed to a restroom next to an outbuilding. It was absolutely filthy. I noticed a slit trench behind the house. Despite the earlier

5. Back in the Foxhole

warning not to use it because it was in the view of our enemy, I pulled down my pants. I immediately heard the distant *pop* and the flutter of incoming mortar round. The first explosion landed far enough away for me to be able to pull up my pants and run around to the side of the house, through the door to safety. I remember thinking that I would have to finish the job when I got back to Company Headquarters. I was sure the German mortar man laughed at that near miss.

Boy Soldier: Recollections of World War II

6. Offensive Advance

In the last week of February we were told to prepare to leave our defensive position the next day in early morning to push through the German defenses. That night a furious artillery barrage was fired at the German lines. The sound of artillery bursts was deafening. The explosions lit up the sky and the hillside across our entire front. Then, of course, the German artillery bombarded our line in retaliation, but it was short lived. We stayed in our foxholes, protected by their depth and the heavy log covering.

At daybreak, we started into enemy territory. There was light, small-arms fire to the left and right of our sector, but none against us. We were shocked at the devastation that our artillery had laid on the enemy. Dead German soldiers were everywhere—many bandaged from previous attacks and artillery fire, but for them it was over. Large numbers of German soldiers elected to surrender rather than flee to their regiment to fight another day.

Frightened German soldiers taken prisoner—being marched to the rear of the fighting, but glad the war was over for them.

Our medics tended to several badly wounded German survivors from our saturation artillery barrage. They had been left behind by their fellow soldiers fleeing from our ground attack. These survivors were then carried by Wehrmacht soldiers, now our prisoners, back to our aid stations.

6. Offensive Advance

The Wehrmacht soldiers were the unified armed forces of Nazi Germany from 1935 to 1946. It consisted of the army, navy, and air force. The Wehrmacht formed the heart of Germany's politico-military power.

Wartime care for wounded enemy soldiers by both sides was not unusual, but difficult to understand when several massacres were reported, such as the murder of 84 American prisoners of war by their German captors near Malmédy, Belgium.

The next day we were assigned the job of taking Hill 320. The summit was the site of a German battalion headquarters that was reported by earlier intelligence patrols. We stopped the night before our attack and dug shallow foxholes—two men to a foxhole. My buddy, Clarence Fuqua, suggested I take the first watch because he was very tired. I agreed, so he covered himself with leaves, as it was very cold, and went to sleep. After three hours, I woke him to take watch while I slept, covered again by leaves.

Suddenly, a sergeant, from another unit unknown to me, awakened me and Clarence, who had fallen asleep during his watch. The sergeant was furious and warned us that we could be court-martialed and even shot for sleeping instead of protecting our position on the front line. Clarence immediately told the sergeant he was at fault—that I had stayed up the first three-hour shift, but he had succumbed to the cold and fell asleep during his watch. The sergeant gave us another warning and then stormed off. I never saw him again and had no knowledge as to why he was in our area, since he was not from Company L.

A few hours later we started up the hill to take the peak. The hill was very steep. A mule team was brought up to carry provisions, munitions, and arms up this hill. The mules did better than we did. Fortunately, when we arrived at the peak, the Germans had left without a fire fight.

That night after we left the hill, we came to a French town called Dambach. We had not fired our rifles for two days. As we approached the buildings at the edge of town, a few rounds of enemy fire came our way. Tired and frustrated, we all hit the ground and commenced firing in the direction where we suspected the Germans were. With no return fire, we went stealthily into town. Two German soldiers came to us to surrender, telling us that a few German defenders left when they encountered the heavy small-arms fire from us as we approached.

Next morning, as we walked through town, we met two girls—one a teenager, the other older—with a three- or four-year-old little girl who started to cry as we approached. The older girls were very frightened, but became relieved when we offered candy and gum. I am sure they thought they would be assaulted by American soldiers.

6. Offensive Advance

Many times during the ensuing weeks of war, we met ladies and girls who were surprised at the attitude of the American soldiers. They had been told that they would be assaulted and raped. Instead, they got candy, gum, and soap.

Boy Soldier: Recollections of World War II

7. Walk to Germany

After leaving Dambach in France, our trek over small roads was detoured. Warned that the road ahead had been zeroed in by German artillery, we detoured into a heavily wooded area.

Suddenly, we heard incoming artillery. We ran forward to escape artillery blasts, particularly tree bursts. Tree bursts would distribute shrapnel like snowflakes in a blizzard. Our assistant sergeant leader, Jerry Babich, was hit in the back of his leg. Jerry was a tough Texan who had lived through the Strasbourg battle without a scratch. Now, he was suddenly writhing with pain but not crying out. He knew that his front line duties were over. The medics tended to him.

When the artillery barrage was lifted, we continued through the forest somewhat disoriented.

We heard the motor and tracks winding through the woods ahead of us. Moving forward, we finally saw a German tank running slowly from left to right with its side towards us, but we were not visible to the crew. We knew our rifle grenades would not dent the tough steel hide of this massive tank, so we called for our bazooka team. The bazooka bearer came, but his ammunition carrier had been lost in the woods during the artillery barrage. So, another rifleman and I fired our rifle grenades at the tank's track, without any results except for alerting the tank occupants that we were there. The tank could not swing his big gun toward us as large trees impeded the movement of the gun.

The tank suddenly reared up and took off away from us, smashing trees and brush. The tank commander was probably fearful of the power of the bazookas that he thought we had. We continued on to the German border lines at Ludwigswinkel.

8. The Siegfried Line

Approaching the Siegfried Line, we anticipated a very tough battle with large numbers of casualties. Many divisions from both the 3rd and 7th Armies were fighting to cross into Germany. We knew the Germans would make a last-ditch effort to keep the Allies out of their homeland.

At each potential gateway to their Fatherland, the Wehrmacht had blown up bridges or set strong defenses against Allied invasions. Their huge anti-tank structures, which looked like concrete dragon teeth, were strong deterrents against swift tank advances. These structures were very evident at Ludwigswinkel, where the 42nd Division was scheduled to cross into Germany. So we knew this would not be the white-sheet surrender pass-through that we experienced in many small towns.

Concrete "dragon teeth"-like structures

Other companies of our regiment had been repelled the day before, losing several men. Hence, our battalion was brought up so a larger group could force its way through the German defenses and into Germany the following days.

Our platoon settled down for the night in a house within view of the large fortifications.

I was assigned to the first two hours of guard duty outside the building facing toward the fortification. I heard footsteps approaching. Before I could challenge the approaching person

8. The Siegfried Line

for the password, I heard a thud. Something hit the ground near me. I realized it might be a grenade. I dove to the ground opposite the sound of the "noise" and boots. Then a concussion grenade exploded. I would have been severely wounded if it had been a fragmentation grenade. As I lay there with my ears ringing and partially blinded by the blast, two of our soldiers ran out of the building. They heard the noise of someone crashing through the brush beyond me, and started firing into that area. At daylight, they found a dead German soldier.

In the early morning, while it was still dark, we moved to a line high on the hill above the Siegfried Line, and dug shallow foxholes for protection. We were given an order to spread orange sheets on the ground just minutes before 7 o'clock. We wondered "Why?," but soon found out when we heard the roar of airplanes coming down the valley. From our high positions on the hill we could see the P-47 Thunderbolts at eye level as they attacked the German Siegfried Line fortifications—dropping bombs and strafing, again and again. The noise was deafening. The ground shook. The vibration was so severe that several of our soldiers vomited and many had impaired hearing lasting for days.

As the bombs were dropped by our P-47 fighters, they exploded, and chunks of concrete and stone sprayed around, forcing us to stay in our shallow foxholes. Unfortunately, while down in the protective hole, I had my arm out on the ledge. Suddenly, I felt something hit my arm. I checked it, and saw that the crystal on my watch had been hit by a flying object. It was shattered. I was concerned that the beautiful Tissot watch, which was given to me in June 1944 by my father, was damaged beyond repair. But, other than the crystal, the watch survived. It probably saved my wrist from minor skin damage.

The fortifications were destroyed. The German soldiers came out of their fortifications with white flags of surrender, stumbling, falling, crawling—completely submissive.

Destroyed fortification structure

That day we walked through the Siegfried Line into Germany without firing a single shot, thanks to the Army Air Forces' P-47s.

I had the crystal repaired in Germany. Then, 60 years later, I gave the still-working Tissot

8. The Siegfried Line

watch and this story to my first grandson, Benjamin Best. Ben still has the World War II survivor (the watch) of the P-47 dive-bomb attack at Ludwigswinkel on the France/Germany Siegfried Line.

Boy Soldier: Recollections of World War II

9. Wurzburg, Germany

April 4th, 1945

After crossing into Germany, we headed towards Wurzburg. Once a beautiful old city, it was now so heavily bombed by British bombers that only one roof in the whole city was undamaged.

After walking through the night, at early morning light we saw the castle overlooking the city. On the wall surrounding the castle there was painted a large "Heil Hitler." Later that same day as we were entering the city we looked back at the castle and saw that the "Hitler" painting had been replaced by a large rainbow of the 42nd Division.

When we arrived at the river, our combat engineers had already built a floating bridge that replaced the very decorative sixteenth-century bridge that had been blown up by the German army.

After crossing the river on the engineers' bridge, we climbed up an incline and walked against a tall stone wall to proceed left to Bahnhoff Strasse. As the first man passed an opening in the wall, he was hit by sniper fire from a church tower in the city. Then, as each man passed the opening, the sniper shot again. I remember taking a deep breath and bending forward. I ran fast across the opening. I heard the expected shot whizzing past. No one was hit again until the last soldier crossing was hit in the neck. Both injured men fell beyond the opening and were attended to by the medical corpsman. We did not stop to eliminate the sniper in the tower because we had a timetable to maintain. We called Company Headquarters and notified its personnel of the sniper, so they could arrange with the Company that was responsible for the church area to eliminate the sniper.

As we turned the corner onto Bahnhoff Strasse following our first scout, we saw two- and three-story apartment buildings on both sides of the street. Immediately we received fire from the second story of a building on the left. Every member of our squad opened fire on the two windows where the shots came from. Both windows were blown out by our rifle fire. When the shooting stopped, two of our men lobbed grenades into the window openings and ran in to the building and up the stairs to find both German soldiers dead. Other soldiers completed the search of that building, but found no other occupants.

We then started a house-to-house search for German soldiers—shooting a few who chose to fight, but capturing several Germans throughout the day.

After clearing several blocks of residential buildings, we arrived at the train station (*bahnhof*). Immediately across from the station was a side street with shops and apartments. While a group of my platoon went into the train station, I turned right onto an intersecting side street. A German soldier was approaching with his rifle held leisurely in my direction. As he raised his rifle to fire, and before I could fire, a shot from behind me knocked him down. I thanked Joe Tappe, who had transferred from the Army Air Forces into Company L just a few days earlier, for his quick and accurate action. That was his first enemy casualty on the battlefield.

In this area our Company killed and captured several enemy soldiers who were mainly Volkssturm (old men and young boys). The older men more often surrendered. The boys preferred to fight.

Back at the train station, we regrouped to send prisoners back to a holding area. During our search we found a large cache of champagne in one basement. We decided to keep it, and later shared it with the tankers who accompanied us and agreed to carry several cases for us.

At dusk we settled into several vacant homes, where we got much-needed sleep. We each took our turn standing guard. However, unknown to us until morning, German soldiers, escaping to the north from our advance, had entered tunnels and had come up behind us for a short-lived attack from the rear.

During the attack, several K Company soldiers were surrounded by surprise and captured by the Germans, only to be shot after capture. When the K Company buddies saw their dead comrades, they went wild, shouting, "Take no prisoners!" They went on a rampage, shooting every Nazi they saw. Our Company continued to take prisoners, but often exchanged fire with Germans hiding in houses.

Toward the end of the day we came upon a structure that looked like a London telephone booth. Upon opening the door we saw a stairway descending down into an underground structure. We heard voices. Thinking they might be more soldiers ready to come up to fight, one soldier pulled a grenade and was ready to throw it into the stairway, but stopped when we heard voices of women and children. We yelled down, "Kommen sie raus!" We were ready to shoot if necessary. Up came a long line of women and children and older men followed by an unarmed

9. Wurzburg, Germany

German officer. When our German interpreter ascertained that there was no one else in the lower level, we let our grenade holder toss his grenade, and then went down to find no one there. We did not know why the German people were down there. I can only assume they left their homes to hide from enemy fire. The German officer was a non-combatant who did not want to fight. We took the officer as a prisoner, and sent him to be interrogated back at a holding center.

Our Company then proceeded out of the city and up onto a ridge overlooking the Main River below. This was a famous wine area, on the side of the hill that led down to the river. It was entirely covered with grape vines and some small farm huts. German soldiers and women came out of the huts with their hands up. Suddenly, from across the river on a high hill, we received automatic firing from anti-aircraft guns that had been positioned there to shoot Allied aircraft. We saw that the guns were lowered and now aimed at us. When the shooting started, the German soldiers and the women began to wave their arms and clothing as if to tell the German gunners that they were also German, and to not shoot at them. The gunfire stopped for what seemed to be a few minutes, but then resumed. It was difficult to run from the gunfire because the grape vines restricted moving up or down the hill. The location of the anti-aircraft guns was too far from us for our rifle fire to be effective. We radioed for our artillery to silence the anti-aircraft guns. Surprisingly, our artillery zeroed in quickly and destroyed the Germans' anti-aircraft guns across the river. After the shooting subsided, we then continued down the hill to the road and to Schweinfurt.

From left to right: Charles Palmeri with Alec Lazar and Norbert Finger after battle

10. Walking to Schweinfurt

That night we gathered with other 42nd Division companies and started our long march to Schweinfurt, the ball bearings factory center of Germany. But, before Schweinfurt, as we approached an open field near the town of Retzbach, Captain Priem, our Company Commander, received information from a forward observer that a stream in a shallow gorge leading into the town of Retzbach was zeroed in by German artillery "88s," and that we should avoid going into that depression if artillery fire should come. Suddenly the ground shook as 88s began to pound into the field. We all hit the ground as the shrapnel whizzed above us. Captain Priem, running upright, ran to his men, kicking them and yelling to get up and move quickly toward the town. He was right. If we didn't move, staying in place would make us a perfect target for German observers. Despite the earlier warning, many of us ran to the shallow gorge because it seemed the safest place below level ground, and below the flying shrapnel. As I was running through the creek bed towards Retzbach, I felt a blast and saw a bright flash that lifted me off the ground. I lost my helmet, but not my rifle. I picked myself up and dashed down the creek bed toward the town, which would be a safe haven from artillery. The German artillery men would not fire into a town occupied by German civilians. Miraculously, except for minor injuries, none of us earned a Purple Heart that day, thanks to Captain Priem.

During the 30-day defense of Strasbourg, which Hitler tried to regain for Germany, the company commander of Company L was killed. Lt. Priem assumed control of the remaining soldiers, leading them to protect the city from the larger German infantry divisions and Panzer tank units. During the last days of World War II, the now-Captain Priem led Company L through several tough fights in Wurzburg, Schweinfurt, and other small towns in Germany. He was always on the front line of every battle. In 1950 he became a battalion commander in the Korean War, where he was injured.

John Harper, who had been running in the creek bed behind me, was astonished when he saw me sitting against the wall of the Gastoff—a restaurant in Retzbach. "I thought you were a goner," he said to me. "I saw you get knocked down by the blast, but here you are, you lucky bastard."

We slept that night in a guest house, and were fed eggs and ham the next morning by the owner—our first hot meal in weeks. I poured myself a mug of what I thought was root beer, but spit it out. It was a dark beer, "dunkel bier."

In the morning we continued our march to Schweinfurt.

Boy Soldier: Recollections of World War II

11. The Luger S/42

April 5th, 1945

Our entire division was advancing to Schweinfurt, the manufacturing center for ball bearings for the Nazi fighting army's equipment and aircraft. The city had been heavily bombed, and we expected strong resistance.

We learned that while most village inhabitants were peaceful, people from larger cities—cities that had been severely bombed— were belligerent, and joined their German soldiers fighting against us.

The day before the final attack on the city, army and division commanders decided to send a large force around the city of Schweinfurt to cut off the escape of German soldiers, and also to attack from the rear to promote confusion and, perhaps, the surrender of the German troops. Our Company L was selected by our battalion commander to accomplish that.

Starting after dark, Company L began a forced march completely around the city on hidden roads. We walked through the night in the rain on slippery, muddy roads, stopping for ten minutes every hour to rest. At one rest stop, they called a halt. As I sat down in the grass and looked around, I spotted a scary companion: a dead German soldier. But even he could not disturb my rest time.

Everyone was carrying extra ammunition for himself or for the machine gun, bazooka, and mortar teams. Most of us walked sleeping—holding on to the shoulder of the man ahead to keep from walking into water-filled ditches.

Eventually—before dawn—we reached our positions, north of the city on a hillside above Schweinfurt. Our line of approach was through the woods. We were very spread out, perhaps 100 feet apart. It was a rather precariously weak line should a large German movement come our way, retreating from the fierce fighting on the streets of the city.

It was quiet in the dense, dark forest and still very early in the morning, but we could hear the guns firing in the city below.

Suddenly, right in front of me—maybe 50 feet —I saw a well-camouflaged dugout with a machine gun pointed right at me. In an instant, I hit the ground and rolled over behind a tree. I saw three German soldiers: one, an officer, he was an older man, and two behind the gun who were young.

I yelled for my buddies, Tom Panasci and Pat Cannon, for support—wondering why I was not a dead man. The Germans must have seen me long before I saw them—they were hidden, and I was standing upright and walking. Why didn't they fire?

As Panasci and Cannon came running through the trees, the officer waved a white handkerchief and yelled, "Nicht schiessen" (Don't Shoot! We Surrender!).

Fortunately for me, these men had had enough fighting and were smart enough to know the war was almost over. That is apparently why they did not fire on the approaching American.

The Germans stood up with their hands above their heads. Only the officer had a pistol—a Luger—which I accepted in surrender and kept. Panasci took the prisoners back to Company Headquarters.

I still own the Luger, and remember the relief I felt when the previous owner surrendered it rather than using it. I thanked God for the outcome of that fighting event.

I later learned that members of Company I, of our battalion, ran into heavy resistance in the city below, and had heavy casualties. So, our assignment to the forced march during the night was a blessing, as our Company L spent the early morning collecting prisoners, escaping the fire fight in Schweinfurt below.

Luger S/42 dated 1936; parts stamped 80 and 780

12. Village of Büchold, Germany

After leaving Schweinfurt we cleared and secured several towns without incident. The residents hung white sheets from their windows, accepting our entry without combat. Most often they were non-combative, but sullen, for in the last days of combat most of the Germans we met were so discouraged with the Hitler/Nazi war campaign that had forced them to lose the fierce pride they once displayed in the mass assemblies in the early days of the Nazi regime. In those final days most Germans blamed Hitler and his cohorts for the shame they had to endure at the defeat of their great country by Allied forces. Knowing the war was almost over, they avoided conflict to keep their homes intact and women and children safe.

So, passing peacefully from town to town, we had become complacent, in fact, a little careless.

It was quiet as we approached the village of Büchold, just northwest of Wurzburg. Most of us were walking, with several riding on tanks. Suddenly a shot rang out and one of the soldiers on the first tank was hit. We all jumped off the tanks and noticed there were no white flags of surrender, an ominous sign. There were no signs of German military anywhere. Then, after we went through the town buildings without incident, my platoon sergeant sent me and Clyde Payton, our Browning Automatic Rifle (BAR) man, to a home at the end of an open field with Dietrich our interpreter, to search the house and outbuildings, and to interrogate the residents.

Dietrich, our German interpreter

12. Village of Büchold, Germany

After meeting a rather large family who told us the German soldiers had left the area, we did an inspection of the house and barn, and then we started to return to the village. But Dietrich was concerned with the attitude of the family members. He thought they were lying.

While walking back across the field, Payton, who I considered to be the best BAR man in the European Theater of Operations, said, "Palmeri, let me use your rifle," and asked me to carry his BAR. He said, "I think I saw a German soldier across the field to the left." He fired my rifle and we saw a German soldier rise up and fall over as his helmet blew off, whereupon the enemy, in large numbers and hiding in a ditch along a small road, started shooting at us. We were about 50 feet from the edge of town. Just before the shooting started, the platoon sergeant with the 1st Platoon came out to see what was happening. He was hit and grabbed my jacket as he fell. My first reaction was to push him off because he was holding me back from my escaping heavy firing, but then I realized he was injured. I half carried/dragged him back to the cover of a building, where a medic attended to him. He had been hit in the groin and thought he had lost his "privates" and starting calling his wife's name. When the medic cut his trousers we saw that he had been hit only in the groin, upper leg, and rear end. Pain or no pain, he was relieved.

Not knowing how many Germans were positioned in the ditch across the field, two of our noncoms decided to attack the enemy using the protection of two TDs ("tank destroyers," which look like a tank but are open-topped). Each TD was to be followed by eight infantry men. When the TD commanders were close to the enemy lines, they saw a huge number of enemy soldiers. Fearing that they could be exposed to a grenade tossed into their open tops, they decided to withdraw. Our tanker turned sideways and tacked back and forth, protecting us until we arrived back at the protection of a building.

The other tank took off back to safety, leaving the infantry in the open field where eight men were exposed to injury. My buddy Clarence Fuqua, assigned to Tank #2, was killed, as were others.

While other members of Company L started firing from our covered position, our observer in the church tower noted that an SS soldier was holding his men in position since one or two had fled the battle. When our sniper shot the SS officer, the remaining Germans surrendered. We captured 60 men. Lieutenant Burr stayed behind to accept the surrender. I was once again amazed at the bravery of our medics who treated wounded soldiers that day—and every combat day.

Our squad leader, Staff Sergeant Fusco, later said that the spur-of-the-moment decision to use

12. Village of Büchold, Germany

the tank attack was foolish, especially since we had underestimated the size of the German troops. The TD cannons and our heavy weapons platoon's mortars should have been used to bombard the German line without any danger to our foot soldiers. This would have brought a quick surrender of the enemy.

Years later, Sergeant Fusco wrote me a letter. Here's what he wrote:

Feb. 21, 1951
White Plains, N.Y.

Hi ya Charlie

I know I'm a stinker and should have answered your letter much sooner I just kept putting it off.

Thanks Charlie for the nicest letter a guy could get! I know there were times when I did things and they didn't seem right, but I did the best I could and tried to be fair.

I hope that some day soon I could talk with you, so if you're ever down this way please look me up. I am not so good in putting things in writing.

I often think of the boys. Do you hear from them. If you have any of their addresses, I'd like to have them.

I've got a few hairs left. I got married Jan. 29, 1950, and it's not bad.

How about yourself. What are you doing. Still going to school.

One of my brothers just left for the army. That makes six of us since World War 2 and another will be leaving in another month which will make seven. Not bad for one family.

Charlie, who took over the squad when I left. Did you boys stay together.

Charlie I always did like you and I know there were a couple of times you thought I was playing favorites, like the first night we were on the line. I told the Lt. that you could not stay there alone. He gave me hell and told me you had to. Then he came down and changed you to another hole. That was one incident. I often think about Fuqua. He had a bad break and I feel responsible for him.

Guess what Charlie I received a letter from blondie, remember?

12. Village of Büchold, Germany

Well Charlie I guess that's all for now. Don't be a stinker like me. I'll be waiting to hear from you.

My very best to you.

Stanley

Charles Palmeri and Pfc. Clyde "Red" Payton

13. Münster Stadtschwarzach

After Büchold

Starting in 1933, as Hitler began his rise to power, hundreds of Catholic priests and nuns were imprisoned in concentration camps for speaking out against the Nazi regime. Two notable priests high in the church hierarchy— Bishop Clemens August von Galen and Bishop Dr. Matthias Ehrenfried—were from the Wurzburg area, and both had been targeted by the Nazis and subject to house arrest for their early, outspoken criticism of Hitler's policies of mass murder of the Jews and Germans who were opposed to Nazi regime, as well as the euthanasia of the sick and elderly.

In von Galen's case, the von Galen family had a deep and loyal love for Germany. The Bishop had actually been in the German Army in World War I. In Germany, Catholic priests were inducted into the army, not as chaplains, but as private soldiers.

When Hitler became Chancellor, Bishop von Galen admired Hitler's early promises to improve life in Germany. But he soon began to criticize Hitler from the pulpit and in letters to government officials and agencies and German newspapers.

It was reported that Hitler wanted to assassinate von Galen, but Joseph Goebbels, Hitler's trusted friend and the Nazi Party propaganda director, suggested that such an action would create a major upheaval in Bavaria, which was very Catholic. Goebbels's job was to present Hitler to the public in the most favorable light, regulating the content of all German media, and fomenting anti-Semitism.

The Bishop had written and distributed through all churches in Germany a written copy of his Sunday sermon condemning Hitler and the Nazi regime for their barbaric treatment of the Jews and others in the concentration camps. The British Air Force somehow obtained a copy of the Bishop's letter and copied it. They dropped millions of copies of the sermon all over Germany in conjunction with their bombing. Hitler was furious, and ordered von Galen to be imprisoned.

13. Münster Stadtschwarzach

After U.S. Forces overtook Bavaria, there was concern that when the Bishop returned to his cathedral, Nazi old-timers might revolt against the Bishop because of his activities against the Hitler government. Contrary to our early concern, there were no disturbances.

Now, 69 years later, Bishop Clemens August von Galen has been beatified—the first step to canonization as a saint.

Bishop Clemens August von Galen

Bishop von Galen was by no means the only Catholic priest to protest Hitler's policies. The concentration camps were full of priests and nuns incarcerated for speaking out against the Nazi regime, especially against the Nazi policy of killing the mentally handicapped; in fact, so many priests were imprisoned there that one of the barracks at the Dachau concentration camp was specifically reserved for Catholic priests, who found themselves subject to inhumane medical experiments and horrific torture.

On April 12th, 1945, our squad of Company L was assigned to reserve duty, particularly to the town of Stadtschwarzach, a few miles from Wurzburg. A probable reason for this assignment was to protect Bishop Matthias Ehrenfried, an outspoken opponent of the Nazi Party who was returning to his cathedral after imprisonment. Like von Galen, Bishop Ehrenfried had been harassed early in his tenure; *The New York Times* reported on April 10, 1934, that the Nazis had "raided" the bishop's palace in response to the recent arrest of another Catholic priest of the diocese for criticizing the government. *The Times'* article went on to report: "The fact that such a demonstration was possible is a striking indication of the intensity of the Nazi-church conflict in south Germany." For defying Hitler, Bishop Ehrenfried would become known as the "bishop of resistance."

I met Bishop Ehrenfried on the day of his return, and had the good fortune to kiss his ring. He was a big man, friendly, and gracious. He blessed us and thanked us for our presence. As a Catholic boy, I always respected priests and pastors and had on a few occasions met our Bishop in Buffalo; I was nervous meeting the top man then.

13. Münster Stadtschwarzach

Bishop Matthias Ehrenfried

But I was not nervous meeting Ehrenfried—he offered us fresh butter and eggs from the cathedral farm. The Bishop was very grateful that we were there when he came home. I'm sure he could be tough on occasion. He had to be, having fought Hitler. Even when in his company I did not know all the facts about the Bishop so easily available nowadays on the internet. That day he told us that President Roosevelt had died, which was news to us. The German residents of Stadtschwarzach came out to welcome Bishop Ehrenfried home without incident.

The Münster Cathedral at Stadtschwarzach, 1945

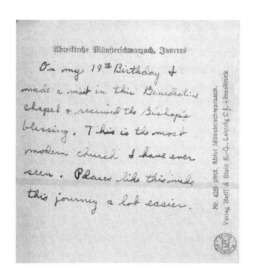

14. Spaghetti and Meatballs

After Münster Stadtschwarzach

My birth date is April 23rd. Sometime in April two packages were delivered to me with my mail. One contained a vicious looking dagger and sheath from my Uncle Sam. Fortunately, I never had to use it with the war's end only a few weeks away. The other box contained something heavy —heavier than the cookies in earlier boxes. When I opened the box, I was amazed. My mom had filled a glass Mason canning jar, carefully packed and sealed, with spaghetti and meatballs. Having been on a K-ration diet since February, with only a few real hot meals since the replacement depot in Le Havre, I salivated just looking at that meal in a glass jar. But, what should I do? We were in a field awaiting orders for our next encounter with "Jerry." Three or four of my buddies saw the birthday gift and eagerly expressed interest in tasting my mom's cooking. I removed the liner from my steel helmet, washed the helmet with canteen water, and started a can of Sterno to heat the spaghetti. After heating the spaghetti, I shared this Italian gourmet meal with four platoon buddies. It was a meal to remember! Later some of the other squad men heard of our feast and came to our position to see if what they heard was true—and if any was left.

Later, I learned that my mother, shortly after she prepared and sent that magnificent meal, had been confined to bed until my baby sister, Theresa, was born in August of 1945. There were many surprises in my military life, but none as exciting as a Mason jar of spaghetti and meatballs...and later the news that I, at 19 years of age, had a new baby sister.

15. Lech River, Egmating

Crossing the Danube/Lech River/Town of Egmating

As we approached Munich, we left the trucks and walked through several villages. When we climbed a short hill and went over the top of the hill, we saw a large flowing river down below. An officer, Lt. Peterson, said, "It's the Danube." I said, "But it's not blue." In fact, the water was brown. We walked to the river's edge carrying and pulling inflated rafts. Each raft had only two oars. So, using our rifles as additional paddles, we rowed across the river toward a large barn. We were prepared to fight upon landing. As the rafts came aground, we jumped off into the shallow water and ran to the barn, ready to shoot, but luckily there were no enemy soldiers in or near the barn. We noticed that the ashes in a tiny cooking stove were still warm, so we knew German soldiers had left recently.

While the pontoon bridge at the Danube River was being built, infantry reached the Lech River and crossed the pontoon bridge under heavy enemy fire.

We continued on, headed for the Lech River. Nearing the Lech we heard rifle fire, and saw our combat engineers building a pontoon bridge while taking fire.

When the bridge was completed, we ran across it, shooting at the enemy. The size of our Company, pounding across the bridge and firing as we ran, caused a number of Germans to flee and others to surrender.

15. Lech River, Egmating

Really, the combat engineers had done the job for us—building the bridge and shooting German soldiers at the same time.

As the infantry crossed the Danube, engineers brought heavy equipment over the Danube and built a pontoon bridge in the swift Lech River.

We then walked to the town of Egmating, the center for a schnapps distillery. We stayed there for two or three days to protect the distillery, and, perhaps, to keep our fellow soldiers away from the schnapps, while the rest of our division was preparing to take Munich and surrounding small towns.

While we were in Egmating, we encountered a farmer who had flipped his large tractor, severely injuring his leg. The people in the town were amazed at the treatment of the wounded man, first by our soldiers, who lifted the tractor off of the injured man, and then by our medics, who transported the farmer to a hospital.

During our time in Egmating, the regiments of the 42nd Division, alongside men of the 45th Division and other army units, captured Munich and the concentration camp of Dachau.

16. Surrender of Munich

The Heroism of Wolfgang Franz Robinow

Wolfgang Franz Robinow was born on August 22, 1918, in Germany, and had, as a boy, lived in Munich. In 1933 or 1934, he and his brother were summoned by their father and told they were going to America to live with an uncle. The boys were not happy about that. They had friends in Munich, and went to school there. They played soccer, and loved their neighborhood. But when a German father in the 1930s gave his sons an order, they obeyed. The father foresaw real problems for his family because their grandparents were Jewish.

Years later, in 1995, Wolfgang personally told me that he had suspected his father had been warned about the Nazi plans for the Jews.

Boy Soldier: Recollections of World War II

Wolfgang Franz Robinow, the U.S. soldier who liberated
Munich

The boys became American citizens, lived in
New York, and, in about 1942, the boys enlisted
in the American Army. Eventually Wolfgang
Robinow was assigned to the 42nd Division
Headquarters Company. His German language
proficiency would be very helpful in interrogating
captured German soldiers. Wolfgang had been
wounded on April 16, 1945, when he saved a
fellow soldier who was wounded in an enemy
ambush. He received a Silver Star for this action.
Wolfgang's brother was killed in combat.

16. Surrender of Munich

When we were gathered and preparing to capture Munich, Wolfgang was so upset that a battle would devastate the beautiful churches, museums, and galleries of this majestic old city that he sought and received orders to enter Munich from our division commander. He was told to take Jeeps and drivers with several armed soldiers, and white flags. On April 30th, 1945, they went down to the center of Munich, the Marienplatz, and to the city hall to seek out the burgermeister (mayor).

Speaking perfect German, 27-year-old Wolfgang pleaded with the burgermeister to surrender the city of Munich to avoid combat, with artillery smashing the city's historic buildings, thus, saving the lives of thousands of German civilians and soldiers of both armies. The burgermeister conferred with the German commanding general, and decided to sign surrender documents, which Wolfgang took to the commanding general of the U.S forces. Although there were a few skirmishes, there was no main battle in Munich. It was the only major Germany city that was not devastated during the war—thanks to Wolfgang Franz Robinow.

While in Munich, a few days after V-E Day, I was guarding a work detail of some old Volkssturm (the People's Army) prisoners. We were in the English Gardens when one of the Germans who spoke English related this story:

Seven or eight days before the fall of Munich, a German underofficer was teaching the Volkssturm members how to use the Panzerfaust (bazooka). After many demonstrations, pointing his Panzerfaust, he said, "Now one more time. Imagine from around that building there comes an American tank...."

From the rear of the class a low voice said, "If you demonstrate one more time, we won't have to imagine—it will *be* there.

I did not know Wolfgang Robinow during my active military life in the Rainbow Division. After the war, Wolfgang obtained a high post in American intelligence, and later worked with a large German company when he moved back to Germany.

At a Veteran Rainbow reunion in St. Louis, Missouri, in 1994, Wolfgang was present. He recalled his involvement in the surrender of Munich, which I have repeated here. He invited the members to accompany him on a Rainbow Division historical tour through France and Germany in 1995. The tour idea was enticing, and I signed up my wife and I. I was looking forward to joining Wolfgang and others to return to Europe. My wife, Carol, could then see where our Division had been during the war in 1945 and 1946. This would also allow us to take short side trips to Mayerhofen and Zell am See.

The entire trip was outstanding. As our host, Wolfgang had made the plans for a magical trip —reserving time visiting Munich, which included a tour and lunch at the Siemens manufacturing facilities; Salzburg, with a special stop to Major General Collins' gravesite for an Honor Wreath Laying Ceremony; Wurzburg, and Dachau. He arranged for all the hotel accommodations, government palace visits, which included special state lunches and dinners, and the opportunity to talk with many German city and state officials.

So, on a Sunday in spring of 1995, the 50th anniversary of the U.S. Rainbow Division's entry into Munich and the capture of Dachau, Wolfgang hosted a reunion of 120 Rainbow veterans in Bavaria, where we were honored by the Governor of Bavaria, the mayors of Dachau and Munich, and the owner of the Hofbrauhaus where Hitler had his first meeting in the early 1930s.

We had similar surprise receptions in Salzburg and Wurzburg. At the Munich Hofbrauhaus we were treated to a huge dinner, beer, and entertainment in appreciation to the Rainbow Division for saving Munich.

Of course, the center point of our tour was Dachau, where over 70 former prisoners attended, some wearing their old striped-pajama prison uniforms. We all gathered at the former concentration camp for a very moving memorial service—50 years after the liberation of Dachau. Some of the former prisoners stood and spoke to the group, once again thanking us for their freedom and life after incarceration.

In the evenings, the 42nd Division veterans and their families would casually meet in the hotel's sitting area and discuss various present and past experiences. At these meetings, Robinow repeated his achievements in Munich and Dachau, many of which I have written elsewhere within this book. One evening he told Carol and me that he planned a trip to Miami, Florida, in the fall. We invited him to take a side trip to stay at our home in Sarasota, which he accepted.

Upon our return to Sarasota, we mentioned our visitor to our friends and neighbors Joe and Maureen Harrison, who had lived in Munich after V-E Day. Joe was a retired Navy Captain who had an assignment of some sort representing the U.S. in some capacity. While living in Munich, they had heard the story of the U.S. Army Sergeant who accepted the surrender of the city in late April of 1945, saving the beautiful buildings and churches and galleries from destruction.

Joe was excited to be able to meet Wolfgang Robinow, which he did at dinner and at our home. It was a magnificent meeting followed by communications by phone and letters for several years.

16. Surrender of Munich

Charles with the Bavarian Minister-President at a 1995
dinner honoring the 42nd Infantry, Rainbow Division

Boy Soldier: Recollections of World War II

17. Dachau

On April 29th, 1945, the day before Wolfgang Robinow's heroic trek into the center of Munich, when he received the surrender documents from the burgermeister, the 45th Infantry and the 42nd Rainbow Division entered and liberated the Dachau concentration camp. The camp was located in Dachau, about 15 miles outside of Munich. This was about two weeks before the end of the war, which occurred on May 8, 1945.

I was stationed in Munich to guard the Volkssturm headquarters. That is where all the records of the young and old "people's army" were housed. Volkssturm soldiers had been recruited late in the war by the Nazis to replace the millions of casualties on the Russian and Allied fronts.

Having heard about the atrocities of Dachau, I accepted an invitation for a Jeep ride to see for myself what had been described to me—what I had then thought was an exaggeration of facts.

On the way, Sergeant Walker, who had been to the camp before, told me that Dachau was the first concentration camp opened in 1932-1933, and, coincidentally, the last one captured and closed by the Allied Forces in 1945.

He explained that in 1932 when Hitler organized the Nazi regime after losing the general election, he was appointed Chancellor by President Paul von Hindenburg, who died shortly after. Hitler's immediate dictatorial actions aroused the concern of many German citizens, who openly expressed their opposition and were then immediately incarcerated into the Munich prison. This prison became so filled beyond capacity that the Nazis took over an old World War I munitions plant just outside a pleasant art colony—the city of Dachau.

So, when anyone wonders how the German people could have allowed the brutality of Nazi leaders, remember that everyone who spoke out or acted against Hitler was put in prison or concentration camps. The first inhabitants of the concentration camp at Dachau were German citizens. Five million were German, French, Hungarian, Polish, Russian, and Yugoslavians.

We were restricted in our walk through the camp. But upon our arrival at the gate to Dachau, the first thing we noticed was the indescribably nauseating odor. Then we got our first view of the naked bodies of men, women, and children piled like firewood five or six feet high—so horrifying, so unbelievable, that I was not sure I could go much further. I was physically sick but determined to continue if for no other reason than to justify my being a part of the great war that had finally stopped this brutal murder of these innocent people.

Corpses at Dachau

As we walked past the furnaces, it was obvious the furnaces had not been used lately because the camp had run out of fuel. The result, of course, was the huge piles of bodies that were awaiting fuel for the furnaces.

Before many other concentration camps were captured by American, Russian and English forces, the Nazis would, in some cases, move the prisoners to the next camp—some forced marched, some in trucks, and many more in railroad box cars. When the railroad cars arrived in Dachau from the prison camp in Buchenwald (the second-to-the-last remaining concentration camp), the locked cars—each filled with 30 to 40 prisoners—were left on the siding; the prisoners inside were left with no water, no food and had no toilet facilities. Most died in the cars.

Corpses in rail cars

In the end, the majority of the over 11,000,000 imprisoned and murdered people were Jews: their only crime was being Jewish.

17. Dachau

When SS commanders heard the sounds of American gun fire in the near distance, they ordered machine guns set up and fired into the cars to kill any possible survivors; this, only two weeks before the war's end. On the railroad siding, 50 or more railroad cars, with their doors now ajar, were filled with bodies.

We were told that only one man survived that brutal railroad car massacre. You can see an American officer helping that survivor in the following picture.

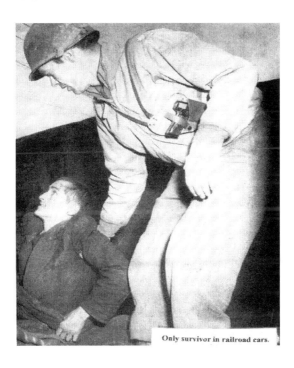

Only survivor in railroad cars.

Suddenly—no, not suddenly—I became less concerned about the thousands of dead prisoners and far more concerned about the prisoners who were still alive—and still suffering. Most of these poor souls, still wearing their pajama-striped uniforms, wandered about barely able to walk on their legs, which were thin as broomsticks. Some mumbled—some cried. Some could not even produce tears. They didn't rejoice. They didn't smile. They knew they were now free but seemed to wonder: "What's next for me?" I wondered what was next for them. Could their emaciated bodies recover? Could they ever lead a normal life?

We brought food, medicine, and help. Many prisoners died after the camp surrendered. Many more would die in the next few weeks.

What we saw and heard about was too horrible. How could men be so cruel—so inhumane? I did not sleep well for weeks after that.

However, some of the German concentration camp guards were different. During the following week, I was on guard in Munich at the Volkssturm headquarters on the corner of Main Strasse when I saw a platoon-sized group of German soldiers who were now prisoners. They were being led—ahead and behind them—by American MPs, together with two former Dachau prisoners in their pajama-striped clothes. I asked one of the MPs where they were going. He said that these were German guards at the prison camp who—at the risk of their own lives— smuggled food, medicine, blankets, and clothing into the camp for the prisoners. The two former Dachau prisoners were there to ensure that our authorities knew that these German guards helped save Dachau prisoners' lives.

But viewing this atrocity gave our mission purpose—which it did when we defeated the Nazis and at least freed some of the prisoners and stopped more atrocities. And then we learned later that Stalin of Russia was also a murderous leader. Obviously, the Russian involvement brought about the defeat of Nazism, along with the involvement of the U.S., England, Canada, France, etc.

Just after our visit to the camp, all citizens of the city of Dachau and nearby villages were required to visit the camp to view the results of the Nazis' appalling disregard for human life. At that time, all German secondary school students were also required to visit a former concentration camp as part of their history education.

As concentration camp prisoners were being herded through the city streets of Dachau to their confinement in the Dachau concentration camp, the citizens of Dachau, once a beautiful art colony, complained about the harsh treatment of the prisoners. The SS Commander asked for a meeting of the complaining group's leaders. Upon their arrival at the city hall, those concerned German citizens were lined up at a building across the street and shot. The bullet holes in the building wall where they stood are still evident, and, per the burgermeister, will be there forever as a reminder of Nazi atrocities.

Many years after the liberation of Dachau, during a reunion meeting in Munich, Wolfgang Robinow repeated an exchange he'd had while interrogating the commanding officer of the Dachau concentration camp.

Wolfgang: "Can you remember how many prisoners you killed while the commanding officer at Dachau?"

Commanding officer: "Can you tell me how many slices of bread you ate in the past five years?"

At our 50th anniversary at Dachau in 1995, we met several former prisoners who came to the reunion. One, Doctor Stanley Fischer, who now resides in Ft. Lauderdale, gave an inspiring speech about his imprisonment as a boy and his rescue as a teenager. He thanked the Rainbow Division for his freedom. Recently I met a Florida real estate broker whose grandparents had been released from Dachau. He told me that they seldom spoke about their imprisonment, but when they did they trembled and cried.

17. Dachau

Above, below: Dachau Concentration Camp, 1995. The sign to the left of the crematorium asks visitors "Please do not write on the walls" in four languages.

My viewing of the horrors of Dachau was limited. Shortly after entering the camp—the combination of the disgusting odor and viewing the stacks of bodies and the 40+8s filled with dead bodies—I threw up right where I was standing and could not continue. I left the camp, and I walked to our jeep outside the gates.

As has been widely reported, General George Patton vomited after viewing the surreal horrors of Dachau, so why should I be ashamed to admit that I could not complete my tour of hell on earth.

18. Jets on the Autobahn

After leaving Dachau we headed to Salzburg, Austria, from Munich. We sped in trucks on the autobahn, one of the first super highways in Europe.

On the way, we spotted several cut-outs in the dense evergreen forest alongside the highway. There, hidden in the trees, were German Messerschmitt Me 262 jet planes. The Me 262s were brought into the war in early 1945. We were told that these planes, with superior speed and fire power, had been hidden in the tree "hangars" to avoid the damage inflicted by our bombers and our fighter planes that were devastating the German airfields. Supposedly, the jet planes had used the autobahn for takeoff and landing.

Seeing this, we were reminded of a strafing we had taken in early April by a quietly approaching German aircraft with no propellers. We had no idea such a plane existed. We also remembered that, after being strafed on another occasion, we watched a jet being chased away by our Mustangs, which were not quite as fast but more maneuverable when flown by our experienced pilots. So, after hoping that the new German jet aircraft would renew the strength of the Luftwaffe, the failure of the jets to control the sky over Europe had to have been a major disappointment for Hitler and his air marshal, Hermann Goering.

19. Salzburg, Austria, First Visit

When we arrived in Salzburg we were billeted in several houses in Ginzling, a suburb with a lake and creek. We met an Austrian woman who offered to wash our clothes—it would be the first time that we had our clothes washed in three months. The pay the woman requested was soap bars, needles and thread, and any cigarettes, candy, and food we had. Afterwards, the citizens of Ginzling, and particularly the frau who washed and ironed our uniforms, were the best-fed Austrians in Salzburg for weeks, and our soldiers were the cleanest-looking soldiers in the 42nd Division.

To top it off, our host had a daughter named "Mousie," who was 17 or 18 years old, a very pretty blonde with a braid that hung below her waist. She was available to guide us soldiers up the mountain to view the magnificent distant Salzburg city, waterfalls, and surrounding hills and lakes. Unfortunately, but perhaps wisely, her mother would not allow Mousie to go out in the evening.

We were not happy to leave Ginzling to head to western Austria and Mayerhofen.

20. Mayerhofen/Patrol

When we arrived in Mayerhofen we all smiled again. What a beautiful storybook village in the Zillertal Valley.

May Day religious procession in Mayerhofen

There were wood chalets with colorful flowers in window boxes, small shops with wood carvers, artists, gift shops, a candy store, violin and guitar makers, and men and women farmers working in the fields singing four-part harmony —everything was neat and clean. The people were very friendly.

One morning after a light rain, there appeared over the valley south of Mayerhofen—not one— not two—but *three* very vivid rainbows. The people said they had seen doubles before, but never three. They took this as a good sign of God's approval of the Rainbow Division in the Zillertal Valley.

Mayerhofen, Austria, 70 km from Innsbruck. The snow-capped mountain in the background is at 10,000 feet. We went up the mountain just before the first day of summer and threw snowballs.

20. Mayerhofen/Patrol

Later, we were astonished to learn of and meet a Jewish resident named Csoker. He had lived in Mayerhofen for years, and, when the Nazi soldiers arrived after Austria surrendered to Hitler, Csoker could have been arrested as a Jew and sent to a concentration camp. At the suggestion of longtime friends, he attended mass at the Catholic Church each Sunday, appearing to be a non-Jewish Austrian citizen.

Rizzi, Csoker, and myself, New Year's, 1946

Surprisingly, every resident of Mayerhofen knew he was Jewish, but no one reported him to the Nazi command. What a tribute to the Austrian citizens of Mayerhofen!

In Mayerhofen we were billeted at Mogel's Hofbrauhaus, a wonderful inn with delicious food, feather-ticked beds, and warm rooms. During our stay there, Company L was called upon to clean up an area near the Italian border where German soldiers did not believe the war was over. They continued to raid nearby farms and homes for food.

Nazis Reported Fighting Yanks

International News Service

LONDON, June 6. — Reports that 300 Nazi SS (Elite Guard) troops were still fighting American troops in Upper Austria were received in Switzerland today from Innsbruck, a Reuter's dispatch from Zurich said.

The dispatch quoted additional reports saying that the United States 42nd Rainbow Division had taken "sharp action" against the outlaw forces and their Nazi leaders.

20. Mayerhofen/Patrol

The local Austrian authorities asked our commanding officer to send a squad of soldiers up the mountain trail to an area near the hamlet of Hintertux to convince the German soldiers that the war was really over. He had arranged for an Austrian doctor, Karl, and his wife, who was also a doctor, to act as guides and to help convince the German soldiers that the war was over. We packed food and beer to take with us to help pacify the outlaw forces.

Very early on June 21, with both food and ammunition in hand, we started up the mountain: 12 armed soldiers, two Austrians, and a German Shepherd named Lady. During our hike, the doctors suggested that when going uphill, it was wise to take short steps—less tiring, especially when carrying arms and food packs.

After passing two hamlets and several shepherd huts, the doctors met the first armed German soldier and quickly convinced him that the war was over. He went up to his camp and returned with several more unarmed soldiers and a sergeant in charge.

While we were prepared to fight if necessary, our persuasive doctors and food, and the appearance of 12 armed American soldiers, convinced the Germans to return peacefully with us to Mayerhofen.

A slow go up the mountain, June 21, 1945

Hoover, Finger, Farber, Lazar, and guide

20. Mayerhofen/Patrol

Charles J. Palmeri, third man from the left

Hudson, Palmeri, Tappe, Lazar, Hoover, Finger, Farber,
Kennedy, and German Shepherd, "Lady"

Boy Soldier: Recollections of World War II

As we walked down a narrow mountain path, the German sergeant walking next to me spoke in fluent English, and asked me where in the U.S. I was from. He didn't know where Buffalo New York, was, but did know of nearby Niagara Falls. He hoped he would be discharged soon so he could get on with his life as a carpenter. He didn't know whether his girlfriend was still available. They had not communicated in over a year. He was from Dusseldorf.

Upon our return, we learned that one of our Rainbow soldiers had been killed by accident. He was lying in his bed when another soldier in a room one floor below had accidentally fired his rifle through the ceiling. What had been a happy return from our successful trip really saddened all the members of Company L. The young soldier had gone through over 100 days of front-line duty uninjured and then died in his bed a few weeks after the war's end.

After our return from our patrol, the doctor and his wife, who had accompanied us, introduced me to their niece, Susan, a very attractive college-bound student who spoke English fluently.

The doctor, who spoke only German, called Susan to be an interpreter. He was very thankful for our patrol's success in the capture of the German soldiers who had been harassing Mayerhofen farmers and their families. He wanted to ask questions about the United States, so the doctor and Susan spent many hours with me in communication about life in the U.S.

Susan and guess who? Mayerhofen, December 31, 1945

After hearing hundreds of Germans and Austrians insist "Me no Nazi," I truly believe the doctor was one of the many loyal Austrians who were opposed to Hitler's invasion of Austria. Then, of course, I was happy to spend time with pretty Susan with her uncle's blessing.

The Company L soldiers who were prepared to fight after the war ended were
Hudson
Kennedy
Tappe
Kuchar
Winter
Ford
Hoover
Palmeri
Lazar
Finger
Farber
Thomson

Company L group photo

20. Mayerhofen/Patrol

In a show of appreciation by Austrian and German civilians...

Just outside of Oberammergau, Germany, where the Passion of Christ is performed every ten years, is a small town where the Catholic Church installed a stained glass window with a rainbow in honor of the Rainbow soldiers who lived there and helped the residents with food and medicines during 1945 and 1946.

In 1995 after our 50th 42nd Division Reunion, I returned to Mayerhofen and stayed at Mogel's Hofbrauhaus, which was now called Mogel's Hotel Neuhaus. I met Joseph Mogel, who was then over 80 years old, and reintroduced myself as a present and former guest at his Hotel Neuhaus. He said that he remembered the 42nd Division soldiers, and commented, "Your soldiers were gentlemen who were friendly and helpful during a rather trying time for Austrians. They were very different than we expected."

Charles on Mogel's Hofbrauhaus balcony, 1945

Charles at Mogel's Hotel Neuhaus, 1995

21. Silver Star

In Mayerhofen, Company L soldiers befriended the local citizens. We provided medical help, food, various provisions, and received gifts and mementos of our stay there.

It was quite disappointing to learn that at the end of the war the Allies had re-divided Austria: the western part of Austria (Innsbruck) was assigned to France; the central part (Salzburg) to the United States; the near-eastern part (Linz) was assigned to England, and very eastern part to Russia. The governance of Vienna was divided between the Allies on a rotating basis.

After Mayerhofen, we were returned to Salzburg, where we resumed training to prepare to fight the Japanese in the Pacific arena. Upon our return, I received an order to report to Division Headquarters to receive a battle award:

the Silver Star. I could not imagine why. I had not been involved in the horrible massacres such as D-Day in Normandy, the Battle of the Bulge in Belgium, or the Mount Casino stretched-out battle in Italy. Our group of replacements was not involved in the Rhine River defense of Strasbourg, when Company L had lost over 50 percent of its men in just a few days. In fact, during my front-line duty, I had witnessed many acts of bravery by men whose actions were not recognized.

The Silver Star
The reverse reads "For Gallantry in Action"

21. Silver Star

HEADQUARTERS 42ᴺᴰ (RAINBOW) INFANTRY DIVISION
OFFICE OF THE COMMANDING GENERAL

22 July 1945

CITATION

AWARD OF THE SILVER STAR

By direction of the President, under the provisions of Army Regulations 600-45, 22 September 1943, as amended, the Silver Star is awarded to:

CHARLES J. PALMERI

42 096 601, Private First Class, Infantry, Company L, 232nd Infantry, for gallantry in action on 8 April 1945, near Buchold, Germany.

In the initial burst of enemy fire during the attack by his company on Buchold, a member of the leading element was wounded. Private Palmeri, leader of an automatic rifle team, left cover, braved the intense enemy fire and carried the wounded man to safety. Volunteering to accompany a tank destroyer, Private Palmeri and his automatic rifleman then left cover to protect maneuvering elements of their platoon. Observing a medical aid man fall wounded, he again left the cover of the tank destroyer and returned with the wounded man. By his outstanding courage and disregard for his own safety, Private Palmeri saved two fellow soldiers from possible death or capture. Entered military service from Buffalo, New York.

HARRY J. COLLINS
Major General, USA
Commanding

109

Boy Soldier: Recollections of World War II

Excerpts from letters to my Dad and Mom:

Sept 6, 1945

Now I have a little news for you. Of course it's not as surprising as what you told me but it is good news in a way.

This morning at 11:16 I'm to appear before Commanding General Collins of the 42nd Inf Division to receive a decoration. I'll write you all about it when I get back because I don't know too much about it.

Sept 7, 1945

Well it's the next day because it rained yesterday and generals just don't have ceremonies on rainy days.

Today was warm and sunny. The band played "The Rainbow Song" & I felt pretty proud as we marched down Heinrich Himmler's lawn in Salzburg. The General pinned the Silver Star on my jacket & asked me how long I was in the Rainbow. Then he said "Congratulations Son."

Now the Silver Star is nowhere near so high as the congressional

21. Silver Star

Medal of Honor & I don't know whether it rates a story or picture in Buffalo news. It might. But one thing is sure. Don't try it until I get the citation orders which will be soon. I'll send them to you. Also the medal.

Sept 8, 1945

I noticed today that my Silver Star is still in the mail clerk's rooms. I guess you won't get it for a while. I sent the general's letter of citation to dad a few days ago. Hope you got it.

Several days after General Collins pinned the medal on to the "Ike" jacket of my dress uniform, I received a notice of furlough to the Riviera in France. What a surprise for me and several others in our regiment.

A short time later, many Company L soldiers, including myself, received Bronze Stars for meritorious combat duty. In addition to his Bronze Star, my company commander, Captain Priem, received the Oak Leaf Cluster for "heroic achievement" in action near Büchold.

THE UNITED STATES OF AMERICA

TO ALL WHO SHALL SEE THESE PRESENTS, GREETING:

THIS IS TO CERTIFY THAT
THE PRESIDENT OF THE UNITED STATES OF AMERICA
AUTHORIZED BY EXECUTIVE ORDER, FEBRUARY 4, 1944
HAS AWARDED

THE BRONZE STAR MEDAL

TO

Sergeant First Class (then Private First Class) Charles J. Palmeri, SK 42 096 601
Military Intelligence

FOR

MERITORIOUS ACHIEVEMENT
IN GROUND OPERATIONS AGAINST THE ENEMY
European Theater of Operations, on or about 12 March 1945

GIVEN UNDER MY HAND IN THE CITY OF WASHINGTON
THIS 16th DAY OF April 1954

22. The Riviera

On my way to furlough, the train trip to Nice, France, with a one-day stopover in Luxembourg and Marseilles, took a week. Many of the railroad tracks had not yet been repaired; hence, we had many detours and delays.

Upon our arrival at Nice we were dispatched to an Army Quartermaster Headquarters. We went to a reception area where we surrendered our old wool uniforms for "new everything," including socks, underwear, and a bathing suit, together with Riviera travel folders describing the places to visit and the places to avoid in the old city away from the waterfront. For those of us who didn't smoke, the ration of cigarettes we received was more valuable than money for bartering use. We were then assigned to a beautiful palatial hotel across from the beach.

When my buddy Clyde Payton (from Mound Valley, Kansas) and I walked into our suite of rooms, we were in awe. As a Kansas kid and a boy from Buffalo, we had never seen such opulence in our lives. So as I was looking around the parlor, Clyde wandered into the huge tiled bathroom, and yelled to me, "Hey, Palmeri, what's this?" I ran into the bathroom, where he was standing over a utility that looked only slightly like a toilet. Expecting to hear an intelligent answer from his New York State know-it-all buddy, I responded, "I think it's to wash your hair." Well, in a way it was, because it was a bidet, something that was not often used or known about in the United States, and not seen again by either of us for many years.

The Riviera offered tours to art galleries, museums, and plenty of pretty French girls as guides. Dance classes were available at the Red Cross, and as much beach time as we wanted. The landscaping was awesome. There were flowers, palm trees, parks, cute little shops, and restaurants.

We went down to the beach and, instead of sand, the surface was all little stones. The officers, however, went to Cannes, where the beach was sand. There was a bonus to our enjoyment on the Riviera. Every day fully dressed girls came down to the beach, each carrying a small bag containing her bathing suit. They would very cleverly switch from dresses to swim suits without displaying any hidden parts of their beautiful bodies. At the end of the day, they would carefully redress while soldiers watched for any careless displays—which never happened. It was a shame we had to leave the Riviera to return to Salzburg. What a wonderful vacation paid for by the U.S. Army.

Charles J. Palmeri, French Riviera, August 8, 1945

It was even more enjoyable when we learned that we would not be going to Japan. We heard a rumor that atomic bombs had been dropped on two cities in Japan. We didn't even know what an atomic bomb was. Later that day when we were on the boardwalk returning from the beach, we saw a large number of soldiers and French civilians in a gazebo reading a printed notice stating that bombs had been dropped on Hiroshima and Nagasaki in Japan. We had no idea of the great devastation that an atomic bomb could have. Later we learned of the subsequent complete surrender of Japan's armed forces in the Pacific area.

What a relief! Some men cried, some were praying and thanking God, and many partied. We were no longer committed to another war— no more killing, and no fear of being killed. Sometime soon we all would be going home to our families and friends and a new future. Wow!

23. Dom zu Salzburg

While living in Salzburg in the fall of 1945, I went to mass at the Dom (cathedral) in downtown. One Sunday a member of our guard detail, Goldkind, asked me if he could go with me to church on Sunday to the 10:30 a.m. mass. I usually went earlier, but, beaming at the idea that I might have a Jewish boy ready to convert to Catholicism, I readily agreed to take him with us by Jeep to the Dom.

When we entered the church, I walked up front near the altar, but Goldkind was not behind me. I looked to the back of the church, and there he was, watching and listening to the Salzburg symphony orchestra that played in the choir loft at the high mass every Sunday. So, it turned out that he came to church with us every Sunday for the beautiful music of this world-famous Salzburg symphony that moved him, but not enough to embrace Christianity.

Oh, well, I tried.

One Sunday, while driving to church on an icy road, the Jeep's hood became unhooked and cut off our driver's view of the road. The car began to spin around and, fortunately, there was no other traffic in either direction. Perhaps Abraham or Moses was unhappy with Goldkind going to a Catholic church on Sunday.

That was the last Sunday of Goldkind's attendance at church, but he did go to the Salzburg's Festspielhaus to hear the symphony on many occasions, and invited me to accompany him. I was amazed at the large number of soldiers who attended and enjoyed the wonderful classical music of Mozart, Beethoven, and other European composers.

Of course, our soldiers spent most of their time listening to and enjoying current, modern music, like "Don't sit under the apple tree," "The white cliffs of Dover"—by Glenn Miller; the Andrews Sisters singing "Boogie Woogie Bugle Boy"; "When the lights go on again (all over the world)," and a German favorite called "Lili Marlene." The music we listened to reflected our light-hearted, post-war mood; we enjoyed popular hits like "Paper Doll," "Apple Blossom Time," and "Thanks for the Memory."

23. Dom zu Salzburg

Corporal Goldkind was a super intelligent young soldier and a fierce rifleman in battle. Living in Salzburg in the army of occupation, he became friendly with respected Austrian officials who were very concerned about the future of their country, particularly because they feared Russian influence and possible future conflict with the U.S. He reported these concerns to U.S. Military Intelligence.

Contrary to rumors voiced in a few recent television reports, Jewish soldiers and non-coms, including Goldkind, were excellent, courageous fighters in Company L during frontline action.

Boy Soldier: Recollections of World War II

24. Camp Marcus W. Orr

This is a part of the history of the Rainbow Division that doesn't appear in any of the Rainbow documents or in any United States reports of significant activity after the end of World War II in Europe.

Just outside of the city of Salzburg, the C.I.C. (Counter Intelligence Corps), in conjunction with the military occupation forces, developed an internment camp named Marcus W. Orr. It was a holding camp, not for German soldiers but for civilians of various nations who had elected to stay in Germany during the war in support of Adolph Hitler and the Nazi regime.

Many citizens of many countries opposed to Nazism were imprisoned in Camp Marcus W. Orr. A large number were from Hungary. In the early 1930s Hungarians had been forced to choose between communism and Nazism. Those who chose Nazism moved to Germany to escape the rising tide of communism in Hungary.

Camp Marcus W. Orr Gate Entrance, November 1945

After V-E Day (Victory in Europe Day) these supporters of Hitler and his murderous policies were arrested and interned at Camp Marcus W. Orr. We were not aware of other similar camps.

Our platoon of Company L was assigned guard duty at the camp with me, Sergeant Charles J. Palmeri, as its leader. After the second week of October 1945, the C.I.C. officer in charge told me that he had been called back to Washington. Until another C.I.C. officer was assigned, the officer placed the responsibility of

24. Camp Marcus W. Orr

supervising all activities at Marcus W. Orr on "Palmeri." That included guarding, receiving and discharging prisoners, record keeping, food supplies, and general maintenance.

120-Man Guard, Company L, October 1945

Guards "at ease," Marcus W. Orr Camp

Guard Tower, Guards, Barbed-wire fence, Prisoners, and
Barracks, Marcus W. Orr Camp, October 1945

Every Saturday a group of 25 to 30
Hungarian prisoners were flown back to
Budapest on a DC-3. Obviously, these
Hungarians did not want to return to
communist-controlled Budapest. One of these
prisoners was Olaszy Sándor, a world-renowned
artist, who had, in 1935, painted a portrait of
Franklin D. Roosevelt that now hangs in the

24. Camp Marcus W. Orr

White House. Another was a beautiful young lady, a princess of Hungarian royalty, who begged not to be returned to communist Budapest. All returnees were certain they would be imprisoned or killed because of their earlier choices opposing communism.

As a sergeant, only 19 years old, I felt deep remorse at having to return these people to Hungary.

An internee, Edith Loitner, a/k/a, "Dynamite"

One memorable internee, Edith Loitner, nicknamed "Dynamite" by the staff because of her size and tough demeanor, had been a secretary to Heinrich Himmler.

125

During the last month of Company L's responsibility at Camp Marcus W. Orr, an army truck arrived with a well-dressed American matron and two servants, along with substantial baggage and a steamer trunk. Baggage of all new prisoners was searched. The lady was upset that she and her maids and their property were to be searched. Despite her protests, she was searched by a WAC assigned to our contingent. This woman was very outspoken about her treatment, for she said she was from a very prominent American family. During the week she was with us, she sent her girls daily to complain about the food, the shabby room, the terrible bed, etc., etc. After the second week, a U.S. army car flying a one-star general flag pulled up, and an army colonel presented official papers to release Mrs. ----- and her entourage, which we happily did.

I never mentioned the name of this prisoner, from one of the most influential families in the U.S. Being the age of 60 in 1945, she has long ago left this earth. I see no need to embarrass her family now. I am sure that her residence in the U.S. was better than it was at Camp Marcus W. Orr.

I have always wondered why she stayed in Germany or Austria during the war. There was plenty of time for Americans to leave Europe before Pearl Harbor. Why was she arrested and put in camp? And why was she released?

24. Camp Marcus W. Orr

When Olaszy Sándor arrived at Marcus W. Orr, he spoke fluent English. Upon his arrival, he asked if he could use a small room in our headquarters building to paint various prisoners. He was given an office where he painted portraits of several Hungarians and one of me.

Sergeant Charles J. Palmeri portrait by Olaszy Sándor

During my session he made a remarkable statement: "In painting, every color is a note. I mix colors and I have harmony, and the finished painting is a symphony. Painting and music are arts—all arts are the same." He said he heard music from my face. But I wasn't making a sound.

Years later I made inquiries at a Budapest art gallery, Kieselbach Galeria es Aukcioshaz, via the internet, to learn more about this famous artist. I learned he studied at the fine arts college of Budapest under Master Painter Rudnay Gyula. Sándor was famous for painting portraits, flowers, and scenery. I was relieved to hear he lived until 1976, having lived over 30 years after his release from Camp Marcus W. Orr and was not a victim of communism in 1945.

During my tenure as sergeant commander at Camp Marcus W. Orr, we had no one escape from the camp, possibly because conditions outside the camp were so much worse in terms of the basics of life: food, clothing, shelter. We did not shoot or harass prisoners. Our guards, who accompanied the returnees on the DC-3s, said the prisoners cried the entire flight, and were treated harshly by the Russians when they arrived in Budapest.

On the day our new C.I.C. officer arrived to take over command of the facility, I received approval to attend the Rainbow University at Zell am See, and was relieved of my responsibility at Camp Marcus W. Orr. I was truly relieved. At the age of 19, to be completely in charge of a camp of this type, not trained to cope with the personal problems of young and old people—it was not an easy task. As an infantryman, wartime killing of enemy soldiers did not bother me as much as this duty.

Vito Rizzi, guarding Nazi POWs who were now custodians, at Camp Marcus W. Orr

Boy Soldier: Recollections of World War II

View of SS Headquarters devastated by Allied bombing,
Berchtesgaden, Austria, April 1946

View from Hitler's "Eagle's Nest," outside Berchtesgaden,
Austria, April 1946

25. Rainbow University

After V-E Day, while I was in Camp Marcus W. Orr, American soldiers began vigorous training to prepare for fighting the Japanese in the Pacific. Army soldiers of the Pacific island battles were brought to Germany and Austria to train us in jungle warfare to prepare for the vicious tactics of the Japanese enemy.

Training for Pacific fighting ceased after V-J Day, but duties for the Army of Occupation continued. Various Division personnel helped in the rebuilding of war-torn cities throughout Europe, helped maintain peace, supplied food and medical supplies, and aided in the search for the Germans responsible for atrocities against non-combatant citizens. While the most notable German murderers were arrested and would be tried at Nuremburg, many fled to

South America and a number remained in Germany, Austria, France, and Italy. We cooperated with the C.I.C. in rounding up these criminals.

(Left to Right) Frankowski, Palmeri, and Thompson, Yankee Hall, Rainbow University

In addition to these and normal activities of military presence, our 42nd Division established

25. Rainbow University

the Rainbow University in Zell am See, Austria. It became a fully recognized college, where Rainbow Division soldiers could earn credits for their future attendance at colleges in the United States when they returned home. A few of the professors were army personnel, but others were hired from American, British, and German universities.

The location of Zell am See was ideal. A large seaside hotel became the classroom center and housing for students and professors. The huge lake offered opportunity for water sports, while immediately across the road was a world-famous ski resort on Mt. Schmittenhöhe.

Charles Palmeri learning to ski, Zell am See

During the winter months, soldiers could skate and learn to ski. Ski equipment and instructions were available for students in addition to joining the Ski Club.

In the winter of 1945, the Vienna Boys Choir entertained us. Then our Glee Club joined the Vienna Boys Choir singing Christmas carols.

Later in life, in Buffalo, when I was in the Canisius College Glee Club, I enjoyed telling my fellow students that I had once sung with the world-famous Vienna Boys Choir.

But—I must admit, when I was a student at Rainbow University in Zell am See, my study time was interrupted by sailing on the lake in the autumn and skiing and skating in the winter, and my school marks were disappointing.

However, learning to ski led to advanced skiing in the snowbelt south of Buffalo years later. As a result of my skiing activity there, a fellow skier, Peter Braun, and I developed a ski chalet village called Craneridge in the town of Colden, New York. Craneridge was a most successful venture, and is now the happy home to over 200 residents—all skiers and good friends for more than 50 years.

I now wonder if Craneridge would have happened if I had not been a ski student in Zell am See, Austria, in 1946.

26. Back to Salzburg

With my guard duties at Camp Marcus W. Orr transferred to another platoon sergeant, and after graduation from Rainbow University, I now had off-duty leisure time on weekends in Salzburg.

Having heard about a circus-type fair in Salzburg across the Salzach River, I went with two of my buddies, Rizzi and Frankowski, to enjoy various amusement rides, Austrian food, and puppet shows. There was no animosity towards American soldiers by Austrians, so we had an enjoyable afternoon. There were, of course, more girls than boys enjoying the day, since most of the young men who had been inducted into the German army were still away from their families. While I was waiting in line to get on a Ferris wheel, I saw a truly beautiful dark-haired girl of 19 or 20 with other girls. My buddy Frankowski approached the girls with his newly acquired German greeting words, only to learn they spoke even less German than he did. They were Ukrainian or Polish, but understood and spoke a little English. Since the non-fraternization rules had been lifted, I decided to try to get acquainted with the dark-haired beauty, who I thought was pretty enough to make it as a Hollywood movie star. However, the language barrier was too severe to allow any meaningful conversation, so they drifted off. When we passed each other a few times later that day, she smiled at me, giving me hope for a future time when we might meet again. Fortunately, we did meet again a few months later.

Company L moved from Salzburg to St. Johann im Pongau in central Austria, where we took up residence in a closed hospital. It was closed because all the patients and medical staff had been moved to a larger hospital a few miles away.

To keep my staff sergeant stripes, I became a Mess Sergeant. Our chef, Ling Louie, arranged to hire three girls from Salzburg to maintain our mess hall and serve. One of these girls was Edie, my earlier acquaintance from the Salzburg festival. We were both too young and unprepared for a serious teenage romance, but we became great friends.

26. Back to Salzburg

Earlier I had written to my mother about meeting a very nice, pretty girl. She wrote back that if I wanted to bring her home to Buffalo, she would welcome her with open arms. In the same letter my father wrote: "Forget it. You have to go to college and get a job!"

Charles (center) with buddies Kennedy and Finger

Boy Soldier: Recollections of World War II

27. Mess Sergeant

In May and June 1946, Company L regiment was stationed in St. Johann im Pongau, Austria. The closed hospital where we were billeted had enough rooms to house additional homeward-bound soldiers on their way to Munich or Salzburg and then home.

A group of 50 or more soldiers from other Rainbow companies, soon to embark to the U.S.A., stopped in one afternoon. Since our own Company L rations were very limited because many of our Company had already gone home, the overnight visitors brought several cases of C-rations (large cases of canned food) for our cooks to prepare for their dinner.

Our head chef, Ling Louie, reported to me that the canned stew smelled bad. It was definitely spoiled—what a dilemma: our own men, plus fifty guests, and food we couldn't serve.

Ling Louie said, "Never fear, I can handle this problem." He prepared a big pot of beef gravy sprinkled with a small portion of ground beef, and then made a couple hundred dumplings and soaked them in the gravy.

Staff Sergeant Palmeri, Chef Ling Louie

27. Mess Sergeant

Explanations for the substitution of dumplings for stew were not necessary. The soldiers gobbled up every one of those dumplings and said it was the best-tasting meal they had eaten in days.

I'm sure Ling is retired now, but I'd bet that he became a first-class chef at a big resort, hotel, or restaurant in New York.

Cathedral of St. Johann im Pongau, Austria, March 1946

28. Major General Harry J. Collins

In late May in 1946, while Company L was still stationed in the former St. Johann hospital, I received my tech sergeant stripes.

Boy Soldier: Recollections of World War II

One Sunday, afterwards, a group of us had just completed a hot round of volleyball after mass and had lunch, when a large sedan with a general's flag drove into our entryway.

As the non-commissioned (noncom) officer in charge, I ran to salute our division commander, Major General Harry J. Collins, who was called "Hollywood Harry," though not, of course, to his face. After my nervous salute, General Collins suggested we do a casual inspection of our facility, which I knew was in excellent order thanks to our strict Company Commander, Captain Priem. Of course, being the site of a former hospital helped our maintenance regimen.

After I apologized for the absence of our officers, we began our tour. Our kitchen and dining room were sparkling. All beds were made, rooms were clean, and hallway floors shining. I could tell General Collins was pleased with the building and the outside grounds.

On the second floor we met with a little surprise. In the Jeep drivers' room, one of our drivers, a corporal, was sitting on his cot with a young girl. The look on his face when he saw the General mirrored mine. I started to raise my voice when the General motioned me to hold up. He asked the driver if he had been on the night Jeep patrol of St. Johann im Pongau. The "yes" reply was enough for General Collins. He commanded "at ease," and told the driver and the girl to stay put. Then he ordered that there be no reprimand for the driver. It was Sunday, and "off duty" time for the driver.

Jeep Driver

Before leaving, General Collins noted my Silver Star ribbon, and asked, "Where did you get that?" I answered, "The small town of Büchold, just after Schweinfurt." He hesitated, then said, "I'll be flying back to Washington in a few weeks. How would you like to fly back with me to the U.S.?"

I waited a second before answering, keeping in mind my sea sickness in January 1945, and

145

then I said, "Thank you, General, but I think I'd like to go back with my fellow soldiers." He smiled and said, "I understand," and shook my hand. Then—my last salute to a general.

As the General was returning to his car he warned me again: "The corporal is not to be reprimanded in any way!" I didn't really know our General, but that day I decided to forget the many patrols he ordered when we were in our foxhole position at Lichtenberg in France.

There is a beautiful cemetery in Salzburg named Saint Peter's Cemetery. This cemetery, formerly reserved for only Austrian nobility, welcomed the burial of Major General Harry Collins, Commander General of the Rainbow Division, in memory of the wonderful works of charity by the soldiers under his direction from May 1945 until late in 1946. Major General Collins had become known as a generous and caring commander for Austrians. The St. Peter's Cemetery was later made famous in the movie *The Sound of Music.*

Also, as evident by his concern for our Jeep driver and friend, he was somewhat of a romantic. After all, he married an Austrian woman who was a member of an Austrian royal family. Perhaps that was another reason why he was allowed to be buried in the Salzburg royal cemetery.

28. Major General Harry J. Collins

I never saw General Collins again, but I did visit his grave in the cemetery in Salzburg, 50 years after the war ended.

From *Pad and Pencil*, the Rainbow University newspaper, January 26, 1946

The day that General Collins pinned the Silver Star on my Ike jacket (July 1945), there were at least 15 or 16 recipients getting the medal that day, and probably more on other days. He could not possibly remember us all individually. When we met in St. Johann in June 1946, it would have been miraculous for him to remember me or to remember the battle at Büchold in April 1945, especially since Büchold was a small occurrence for the 42nd Division on a day when other 42nd Division companies were active in Nuremberg, Fürth, and many other small towns like Büchold.

29. Goodbye to Austria

During my time in the occupation of Austria, I met a few girls who became good friends, including "Mousie," whom I met in Salzburg just after our arrival in Austria, and Susan, whom I met in Mayerhofen after being introduced by her aunt and uncle, our guides in the after-war patrol.

Both girls were really pretty, smart, English speaking, and exceptionally pleasant. Both had mothers who trusted me, a young American soldier, to spend time with their daughters. I did nothing to upset that trust, even though the non-fraternizing ban had been lifted.

However, at the fair in Salzburg, I first met Edie, and realized she was someone special. I felt an immediate spark. How fortunate that we crossed paths again in St. Johann im Pongau two months later.

Charles Palmeri in tent city

As a mess sergeant, I spent many duty hours with the three girls that our chef had hired for kitchen duties. They were exceptionally good and loyal workers. Soon, I became more attracted to Edie through her beauty and her warm, friendly smile. I found myself spending considerably more non-duty hours with her. My background as a young seminarian had given me no opportunity to experience romance, but my love for this beautiful girl became overwhelming. She was affectionate and very patient.

Edie in the mess hall

Edie by the pool

Edie learned English very quickly. She had been an eager student, and wanted to know everything about America. Together we were able to tell each other in simple terms about our past —in her case, particularly being separated from her mother and brother in a replacement center in Germany, and her failure in trying to find them.

Edie with her dog

Then came the day every soldier looks forward to: "going home."

As anxious as I was to return to Buffalo and begin my future—college and civilian work—I was a little sad. While most of my combat buddies had already been discharged, a few friends were still there waiting on the closing day for the 42nd Division, which was imminent.

29. Goodbye to Austria

I realized that I would miss Edie. She had become an important part of my life, but there was nothing I could do to continue our relationship, and she had no address to receive letters. She had my address, but I never received any mail from her.

I didn't tell her I was leaving because I couldn't imagine how I would handle the "goodbye forever" scene.

As I was climbing on the truck that would take us to the railroad station, I looked at the front entrance of our office and saw Edie standing on the front steps, all dressed up in blue and yellow like she was going to a cocktail party. I jumped off the truck and ran to her. Both of us were crying and hugging for one last forever kiss. When my truck pulled up, the driver waited a minute, then blew the horn. As we drove away, we waved to each other, and I cried. I would never see Edie again.

MEA CULPA

There are many tragedies in post-war times that are rarely considered in the books of history, not only after World War II but after all war times. This was more significant during the World War II occupation of England, Italy, Germany, and Austria. Many thousands of young men, 18 or 19 years old, had experienced only flirtations and puppy love before they were thrown into the demanding, frightening adventures of war. Then, following V-E Day in the relaxing air of a foreign land, meeting pleasant citizens—especially pretty young girls who had been teenagers when the war began— these young men found romance. It was startling, overwhelming, and intriguing, but to what end? The girls, who are probably more intensely involved, are one day abandoned by the handsome uniformed young men who returned to the U.S. with no chance of future communication.

While I was in the Salzburg railroad station waiting for the train to take us soldiers to Le Havre and then on to our ships to New York, a young girl approached me with an envelope. "Do you know Peter Harringten? He is a Rainbow soldier on his way to America. If you do not, would you try to find him on the boat or later in the U.S.?" I replied, "I do not know him, but I'll try to find him." Obviously, I tried unsuccessfully. Here is the original letter, as well as the typed-out version, which follows. Read it. It is a heartbreaker.

29. Goodbye to Austria

Frankenberg, January 7th 1846.

My dear Peter!

We arrived Frankenberg very well. But as I leaved Salzburgh my heart was broken. Peter, I shall not remain in Frankenberg for a long time because I must go to Innsbruck to begin my new work. Dear Peter, I shall try all to see you again before you go to America. My heart says I must see you again. But it is not easy for me because a foreign man has to fix over my ... I ... you with all my heart. Please, sent me your American-adresse in your letter. It is possible that my chief (me) don't let go me to you and what I have then - all nothing. I cannot see you again and I have no adresse from you. Please, if you really love me, sent me your adresse. You know that we will ... in the abroad and to London too. Peter, can you feel, how dismal my heart is? - My thoughts are alway by you, my only darling. Do you think sometimes on your Eve too? Or have you forgotten me because Risoli is by you again? O Peter, I think on the old days and I am so happy, but now it grows ... round me. But the thought on you and a letter from you make me happy. - But I cannot believe that you can ... on me if you go at home in the next month. I think it will be continue a long time until ... person can go to America. The USA - ... don't take a foreigner if he has ...

155

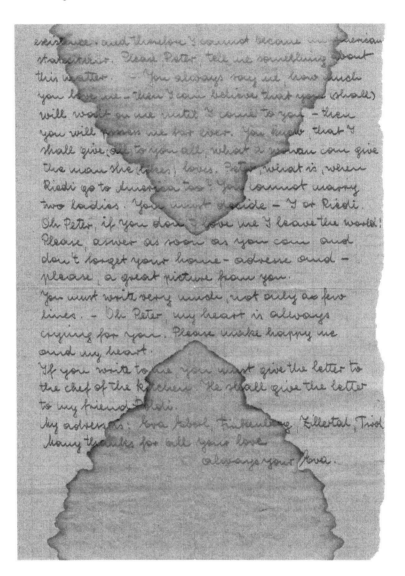

29. Goodbye to Austria

Finkenberg, February 7, 1946

My dear Peter!

We arrived Finkenberg very well. But as I leaved Saltburgh my heart was broken. Peter, I shall not remain in Finkenberg for a long time because I want to go to Kursbuch to begin my new work.

Dear Peter, I shall try all to see you again before you go to America. My heart says: I must see you again! But it is no easy for me because a foreigner now has to fix over me, therefore I ask you with all my heart: please sent me your American-address in your letter. It is possible that my chief (me) don't let go me to you and what I have there-all us thing.

I cannot see you again and I have no address from you. Please, if you really love me, sent me your address. You know that we will rise in the abroad and to London too. Peter, can you feel how dismal my heart is? My thoughts are always by you, my only darling. Do you think sometimes on your Eva too? Or have you forgotten me because Risdi is by you again? Oh Peter, I think on the old days and I was so happy. But now is gray fog round me. But the thought are you and a letter from you make me happy. – But I cannot believe that you can wait on me, if you go at home in the next month, I think, it will be continue a long time until civil persons can go to American. The USA –State don't take a foreigner if he has no experience and therefore I cannot become an American state citizen.

Please Peter, tell me something about this matter. – You always say we have much you love me-then I can believe that you (shall) will wait on me until I come to you. – then you will possess me forever. You know that I shall give you (all) to you all, what a woman can give the man she (likes) loves. Peter, what is, where Risdi go to American too? You cannot marry two ladies. You must decide – I or Risdi. Oh Peter, if you don't love me I leave the world! Please, answer as soon as you can and don't forget your house – address and – please, a great picture from you.

29. Goodbye to Austria

You must write very much, not only a few lines. – Oh Peter, my heart is always crying for you! Please make happy me and my heart.

If you write to me, you must give the letter to the chef of the kitchen. He shall give the letter to my friend Poldi.

Many thanks for all your love

Always your Eva

Harold Ortman from West Seneca, New York (a Buffalo suburb), accompanied me to Europe in January 1945. Both of us were assigned to Company L throughout the war and the Army of Occupation. We were now ready to return home from Le Havre, France, on a troop ship called the *Sea Tiger*. After our discharge at Fort Dix and a brief visit to Manhattan to see the Rockettes, we rode in a comfortable railroad car during the rest of our journey home.

Harold Ortman and Charles, on the way home

Epilogue: July 1945, Home

After a year in the U.S. Army of Occupation, I returned to Buffalo and graduated from Canisius College in 1950 with a BBA degree.

Mom, brother Vincent, Charles, Dad

After college, during my first years of civilian life, I joined the U.S. Army Reserves and was commissioned as a 2nd Lieutenant in the Counter Intelligence Corps (C.I.C.).

In 1953 I started and managed a car rental business in Buffalo, before moving on to a large millwork company to introduce new products for home construction. This led to management of a large land development construction company, and then the start-up of my own land development company in the Buffalo area.

After a move to the Atlanta, Georgia, area, I returned to the millwork business with Combustion Engineering's Morgan Millwork.

In 1978 I moved to Sarasota, Florida, to begin a very successful career as a commercial Realtor®, which continues today (2020) at the age of 93.

In 1950 I married Norma Cosentino in Buffalo and raised three daughters: twins Karin and Karla, and Janine. Norma succumbed to cancer in 1991. Two years later I married Carol Rodak-Huber, and added Carol's daughter, Cheryl, and Cheryl's husband, Dale, and their two sons, Brett and Cameron, to the make-up of our blended family.

Together, Carol and I are partners in a successful commercial and residential real estate business.

Epilogue: July 1945, Home

Rep. Vern Buchanan presenting me with the American flag that flew over the United States Capitol on July 22, 2016, the 75th anniversary of my receiving the Silver Star.

My major accomplishments in civilian life are:

1. Seven grandchildren and 13 great-grandchildren
2. Establishing the first auto rental airport office in Buffalo, NY, in 1950
3. Introduced pre-hung doors in 1954 to the home building industry in New York, Pennsylvania, and Ohio
4. Development of a new community, Ransom Oaks, in Amherst, NY, with Caldwell Development Corp.
5. President of Niagara Frontier Builders Association
6. Craneridge, a ski chalet community with round lots in Glenwood, NY, with partner Peter Braun
7. Gulfside Beach Club, a condo conversion in Nokomis, FL, on the Gulf of Mexico
8. Commercial real estate broker from 1983 through today

Afterword

After my return home to Buffalo, I did not carry battle baggage with me. I was too young to give much thought to the political or the philosophical implications of war. I focused on life: college, sports, and planning a career.

Before the war, I had been seriously considering entering the priesthood. I had attended a strict Catholic school from an early age, but finally had to admit that it wasn't for me: I liked pretty girls too much. When I told my father I was not going to pursue the priesthood, my mother, who was in the kitchen and could overhear our conversation, broke out into sobs. I did meet with my priest, though, and explained my feelings. He told my father that I was a "good boy" and would become a good soldier. But as far as my war experiences went, I did not go to confession to ask forgiveness about anything I did in the war—my conscience was clear.

My immediate concerns were with my family. Dad had several repair jobs for me to complete in our new, but very old, house. In return, I could use his new car on dates in the evening or to the beach in Canada on weekends.

I spent time with my two cousins, John and Jim, who were also veterans, and also with other veterans I knew. We very seldom discussed the war except for humorous events. I had my photo album and clippings, which I reviewed from time to time, but even my daughters did not know about my role as a soldier. I often thought about Dachau, but didn't discuss it until I was in my mid 80s, when I was asked to participate in panel discussions at schools, church, and club functions. Some of my involvement in those discussions ignited my memories of seeing Dachau, as did my 1995 return trip to Dachau with the 100 Rainbow Division Veterans on our 50-year Anniversary Tour.

It was disturbing to have our military involved in Korea in 1950. Fortunately, our Army Reserve unit was never called to fight in Korea, but my former company commander, Capt. Priem, did fight in Korea. He described to me his involvement in Korea when I visited with him in Monterey, CA, years later.

When our country was preparing to fight in Iraq, I sent a long handwritten letter to President George W. Bush asking him to consider carefully before plunging our nation and our troops of young men into such a disruptive, life-altering situation. He did not reply.

Reports of the deaths of our men and women in Vietnam, and now Iraq and Afghanistan, have been very disturbing.

What happened to "the war to end all wars"?

Charles J. Palmeri, September 2019

P.S. As I sit back and reflect on the book I've just completed, I have given a great deal of thought to the letter to Peter Harringten, the letter that I included in my book, the letter that I still have. I've decided that there is no reason to cause any disruption to Peter's family after all these years, and so I will donate the letter to the Chapman University Center for American War Letters Archives.

And, I will continue to try to locate a member of 2nd Lieutenant Antonio J. Manniello's family, so that someday the Italian-American dictionary that he so treasured and wanted me to protect while he was on night patrol can be returned to where it belongs.

Boy Soldier: Recollections of World War II

For further reading.

For more information about the history and accomplishments of the 42nd Infantry, Rainbow Division, I encourage you to visit www.rainbowvets.org, and read *Reveille*, the newsletter of the 42nd.

Below is a list of several books that I recommend highly.

Hell Before Their Very Eyes: American Soldiers Liberate Concentration Camps in Germany, April 1945, by John C. McManus

The Liberators: America's Witnesses to the Holocaust, by Michael Hirsh

Dachau 29 April 1945: The Rainbow Liberation Memoirs, edited by Sam Dann

For a riveting, minute-by-minute account of the official liberation of the Dachau concentration camp, this book is the gold standard: *Surrender of the Dachau Concentration Camp 29 APR 45: The True Account,* by John H. Linden.

Photo credits.

Photo credits.

Photos found on pages 20, 26, 34, 36, 64, 65, 73, 74, and 75 were originally published in *2nd "Rainbow" Infantry Division A Combat History of World War II*, copyright 1946, by the Army & Navy Publishing Company of Baton Rouge, LA. Unless otherwise noted, all other illustrations and photographs are from the personal collection of Charles J. Palmeri.

Made in the USA
Columbia, SC
22 March 2022

57961355R00104